OECD Public Governance Reviews

Empowering Youth and Building Trust in Jordan

This work is published under the responsibility of the Secretary-General of the OECD. The opinions expressed and arguments employed herein do not necessarily reflect the official views of OECD member countries.

This document, as well as any data and map included herein, are without prejudice to the status of or sovereignty over any territory, to the delimitation of international frontiers and boundaries and to the name of any territory, city or area.

The statistical data for Israel are supplied by and under the responsibility of the relevant Israeli authorities. The use of such data by the OECD is without prejudice to the status of the Golan Heights, East Jerusalem and Israeli settlements in the West Bank under the terms of international law.

Note by Turkey
The information in this document with reference to "Cyprus" relates to the southern part of the Island. There is no single authority representing both Turkish and Greek Cypriot people on the Island. Turkey recognises the Turkish Republic of Northern Cyprus (TRNC). Until a lasting and equitable solution is found within the context of the United Nations, Turkey shall preserve its position concerning the "Cyprus issue".

Note by all the European Union Member States of the OECD and the European Union
The Republic of Cyprus is recognised by all members of the United Nations with the exception of Turkey. The information in this document relates to the area under the effective control of the Government of the Republic of Cyprus.

Please cite this publication as:
OECD (2021), *Empowering Youth and Building Trust in Jordan*, OECD Public Governance Reviews, OECD Publishing, Paris, *https://doi.org/10.1787/8b14d38f-en*.

ISBN 978-92-64-94291-2 (print)
ISBN 978-92-64-37131-6 (pdf)

OECD Public Governance Reviews
ISSN 2219-0406 (print)
ISSN 2219-0414 (online)

Photo credits: Cover © John Lund/Blend Images/Getty Images.

Corrigenda to publications may be found on line at: *www.oecd.org/about/publishing/corrigenda.htm*.
© OECD 2021

The use of this work, whether digital or print, is governed by the Terms and Conditions to be found at *http://www.oecd.org/termsandconditions*.

Foreword

With a share of 36%, youth (12-30 year) represent more than one-third of the total population in Jordan. Public governance can support youths' transition to an autonomous life and provide opportunities for their full participation in economic, social and public life. The COVID-19 pandemic has hit young people in Jordan hard and has underscored the importance of ensuring that young people have access to high-quality public services and opportunities to participate in decision making.

This report provides an analysis of the governance arrangements put in place by the government of Jordan to deliver youth-responsive policy outcomes, focussing on five areas: 1) Jordan's National Youth Strategy 2019-25, 2) institutional capacities of the Ministry of Youth, 3) governance tools to mainstream youth considerations in policy making and service delivery, 4) youth participation and representation in public life and 5) youth-responsive legal frameworks. The report helps policy makers -- notably the Ministry of Youth, other line ministries, government agencies and their partners -- strengthen administrative capacities to deliver policies, programmes and services that are responsive to the diverse needs of youth. Ultimately, it should help the government empower youth and build trust in public institutions.

The report is based on replies to the OECD Youth Governance Survey conducted by the Ministry of Youth as well as several fact-finding missions carried out between 2017 and 2020 in Jordan. Preliminary findings and recommendations were discussed with the Project's Steering Committee, most notably the Discussion Paper "Towards a new partnership between government and youth in Jordan" in June 2017, and the Key Findings Paper "Building administrative capacity to empower youth in Jordan" in March 2020 in Amman. The Steering Committee brings together youth stakeholders from nine line ministries, entities affiliated to the Royal Court, universities, NGOs and international partners. The report also benefited from focus group discussions with governors, youth directors and young members of youth centres at subnational level, notably in Greater Municipality Amman and the governorates of Aqaba, Krak, Irbid, Mafraq and Tafileh. Moreover, the report includes insights from youth stakeholders from Jordan, the MENA region and OECD countries gathered during several technical workshops, high-level conferences and the MENA-OECD regional youth conferences in 2017 in Morocco and 2018 in Tunisia.

The report draws on the evidence gathered by the Public Governance Committee (PGC), the Regulatory Policy Committee, and PGC sub-bodies as well on OECD Recommendations in the area of public governance. It is also aligned with the OECD Youth Action Plan (2021). It integrates relevant insights and good practices from the OECD report (2020) *Governance for Youth, Trust and Intergenerational Justice: Fit for all generations?* and the OECD Policy Response (2020) "COVID-19 and Youth: Response, recovery and resilience". It compares current practices in Jordan against international benchmarks, with a focus on OECD countries and economies in the Middle East and North Africa (MENA) region. It also draws on the work in Jordan on youth inclusion implemented by the OECD Development Centre until 2018.

This report is part of the regional project "Youth in Public Life: Towards open and inclusive youth engagement", which supports the governments of Jordan, Morocco and Tunisia in fostering a more active and inclusive engagement of young people in public life and in delivering youth-responsive policy outcomes, complementing work conducted by the OECD with the government of Jordan on open government and gender equality in public life. The regional project is financially supported by the MENA

Transition Fund of the G7 Deauville Partnership and is implemented by the MENA-OECD Governance Programme, as per the priorities outlined in the 2016 Tunis Declaration and the 2021 MENA-OECD Ministerial Declaration. In the context of this regional cooperation, the OECD also published the reports "Empowering youth and building trust in Morocco" and "Empowering youth and building trust in Tunisia" in June 2021.

Acknowledgements

The report was prepared by the OECD Public Governance Directorate (GOV), headed by Elsa Pilichowski. It was developed under the strategic direction of Martin Forst, Head of the Governance Reviews and Partnerships Division in GOV, and of Miriam Allam, Deputy Head of Division. The report and the work on youth empowerment and intergenerational justice is co-ordinated by Moritz Ader.

Mai Hosny (Chapter 1, 3 and 5), Moritz Ader (Chapter 2) and Pietro Gagliardi (Chapter 4) co-authored the report and were responsible for the data collection and analysis. Valuable feedback was received by Charlotte Denise-Adam and Amira Tlili (Governance Reviews and Partnerships Division), Michael Jelenic, Paulina Lopez Ramos and Claire Mc Evoy (Open and Innovative Government Division) and Meeta Tarani (Policy Coherence for Sustainable Development Goals Division). Support in the data-collection and validation process was provided by Rimaz Abu-Zeyad, Stephanie Attil, Lamia Benhoummane, Caroline Mina, and Aichetou Taffa. Ciara Muller with the support of Francesca Romani prepared the manuscript for publication and controlled the quality.

The authors express their gratitude towards the Ministry of Youth for completing the OECD Youth Governance Surveys, notably Minister of Youth, H.E. Mohammad Salameh Faris Nabulsi, and extend their gratitude to former Ministers Dr. Faris Abdel-Hafez Braizat, Dr. Mohammad Abu-Rumman, Makram Al Qaisi, Bashir Ali Al-Rawashdeh, Eng. Hadeetha Khreshah and Rami Al-Wreikat. They are grateful to Secretary-General Hussein Jbour, and former Secretary-General Thabet Al-Nabulsi and Satam Awad. They thank all employees that participated in the interviews and data collection process, notably Jabr Ereaqat, Dr. Salam Al Hassanat, Dr. Yassein Al Hulayel, Hasan Khawaj and Ayat Alodat.

They express their thanks to the Ministry of Planning and International Co-operation for representing Jordan in the MENA Transition Fund of the G7 Deauville Partnership, in particular Nizar Awad, Sameer Al-Attar, Marwan Al-Refai, Zeina Toukan and Nasser Al-Zou'bi. They also thank the Governors of Aqaba and Mafraq and Youth Directors and representatives from the youth centres in Greater Amman Municipality, Karak, Aqaba, Tafileh, Irbid and Mafraq for their inputs during the fact-finding missions and focus group discussions.

The report benefitted from comments of the members of the Steering Committee on previous draft documents in May 2017, July 2018 and March 2020 respectively. The authors are grateful to the Ministry of Education (Dr. Hisham Qawasmeh), Health (Ibrahim Kana'n, Dr. Riham Jabour Majali), Higher Education, Interior (Mr. Muhammad Al-Awamreh), Labour (Ahmed Al-Kharabsheh), Municipality Affairs (Rowaida Habahba, Rakez Al-Kalaelah), Political and Parliamentary Affairs (Qussi Al Zoubi, Dr. Ali Al-Kawaldah), Public Sector Development (Fayez Alnahar), and Social Development (Dr. Loay Al-Assaf). They are also thankful to All Jordan Youth Commission, Crown Prince Foundation, Department of Statistics (Ikhlas S. Aranki), El Hassan Youth Award (Samer Al Keldani), Higher Population Council, Jordanian Hashemite Fund for Human Development, Jordanian National Commission for Women, Jordan River Foundation, King Abdullah II Funding Foundation for Development, King Hussein Foundation's Information and Research Center, National Council for Family Affairs (Khitam Al-Utaibi), Queen Rania Center for Entrepreneurship, and Wafa Bani Mustafa (MP). They thank Al Hayat Center (Dr. Amer Bani Amer, Osama

Muhsen, Mohammad Al-Tamimi), Leaders of Tomorrow (Sami Hourani), Ruwwad for Development (Moath Al-Akaylah), Partners Jordan (Rasha Abdel Latif, Sana Yassin) and Dr. Mustafa Heilat.

They wish to warmly thank all OECD peers that participated in the fact-finding missions and focus group discussions notably the European Youth Forum (Tina Hočevar), Slovenia (Dr. Peter Debeljak), Germany (Tim Schrock), Sweden (Sanna Hansson), Tunisia (Maha Trabelsi) and United Kingdom (Shah Mahmud). They are also grateful to the participants of Jordan in the MENA-OECD Regional Youth Conference in 2017 and 2018 (Arwa Aljarhie, Arafat Awad Mahmoud, Mohammad Habarneh, Rasha Al Katheeb, Hussein Al-Sarayreh, Ragheb Shraim, Ali Sider, Hamza Al Tarawneh, Sanah Yassin).

They would like to thank all G7 countries for the financial support provided through the MENA Transition Fund of the G7 Deauville Partnership, notably Canada (Amal El-Atifi, Christopher Johnston), France (Ambassador David Bertolotti, Sophie Bel), Germany (Dr. Mark Erbel, Dr. Bernd Kuzmits, Jaime Sperberg), Italy (Ambassador Fabio Cassese, Ambassador Giovanni Brauzzi, Valeria Romare, Dr. Marco Salaris), Japan (Katsuhiko Araike), United Kingdom (Ambassador Edward Oakden, Tonaina Ngororano, Caroline Morris, Dima Obeidat) and United States (John Hishmeh). They are also thankful to the Danish Arab Partnership Programme (Anne Kahl), the Delegation of the European Union to Jordan (Jacob Arts, Barbara Engelstoft, Michael Steffens), Netherlands (Rawan Da'as, Nawal Qutub), Spain (Vicente Ortega, Mercedes Cornejo Bareas), Sweden (Izabella Eriksson) and Switzerland (Ambassador Lukas Gasser, Alexandra Häfliger, Manuela Sells-Rohrbach).

Finally, they wish to thank the European Center for Electoral Support (Mario Orru), National Democratic Institute, Netherlands Institute for Multiparty Democracy (Rami Adwan), Norwegian Refugee Council (Emmar Bonar), UNDP (Majida Al-Assaf, Mais Abdallat, Diana Jreisat), UNESCO (Dania Dirani), UNFPA (Bothaina Qamar, Leana Islam), UNICEF Regional Office (Besan Abdelqader, Veera Mendonca, Giorgia Varisco), UNICEF Jordan Office (Dina Al Jamal), USAID (Courtney Babcock, Omar Al Daoudieh) and World Bank (Tobias Lechtenfeld, Sherien Skrikorian).

Table of contents

Foreword	3
Acknowledgements	5
Acronyms and abbreviations	10
Executive Summary	12
1 Assessing the situation of youth in Jordan	**15**
National trends driving the perception of government	17
Access of youth to public services and participation in public life	21
Outline of the report	25
References	26
2 A joint vision for youth in Jordan: The National Youth Strategy 2019-25	**30**
Investments into national integrated youth strategies pay off	32
Reinforcing capacities to steer strategy, coordinate and track progress	34
References	47
3 Building administrative capacity to deliver for youth in Jordan	**51**
Organisation of youth affairs at the central level	52
Building skills for youth-responsive policy making and programming	55
Financial resources for youth programming are scarce	58
Coordination across Ministries and Levels of Government	61
Youth Affairs at the Subnational Level	63
Mainstreaming youth considerations in policy making and service delivery	64
References	67
4 Youth participation and representation in public life in Jordan	**72**
A strong relationship between youth and public institutions	73
Youth express higher trust in government than other age cohorts but less than in the past	73
Promoting an enabling environment for youth participation	75
Developing new formats for youth non-institutionalised participation	76
Encouraging young people to go to the ballot box	77
Youth remain under-represented in Jordanian public institutions	80
Including youth in the policy cycle	83
Young volunteers: builders of resilience	87
References	90

5 Legal frameworks to empower and protect youth in Jordan — 96
Defining the rights, roles and responsibilities of youth — 97
National youth laws can help pursue a co-ordinated approach — 97
Jordan's endorsement of children and youth rights — 99
Minimum-age requirements in Jordan — 100
References — 104

Tables

Table 2.1. NYS 2019-25: Themes and strategic objectives — 34
Table 2.2. OECD Assessment Framework of National Youth Strategies — 35
Table 3.1. Bodies with formal responsibility for youth affairs in selected MENA governments, 2021 — 52
Table 3.2. Inter-ministerial coordination in selected MENA countries, 2020 — 63
Table 5.1. Legal frameworks stipulating minimum ages for political participation in Jordan, 2021 — 102

Figures

Figure 1.1. Demographic composition of Jordan by age cohort, 2020 and 2030 (forecast) — 16
Figure 1.2. Main concerns raised by survey respondents in Jordan, 2019 — 18
Figure 1.3. How respondents perceive the economic situation and corruption in Jordan, 2006-2018 — 19
Figure 1.4. Jordan Corruption Index, 2000-2020 — 20
Figure 1.5. Share of youth in Jordan considering to emigrate, 2006-2018 — 21
Figure 1.6. Share of youth not in education, employment or training, Jordan, (2017-2019) — 22
Figure 2.1. National Youth Strategies in the MENA region — 32
Figure 2.2. Strategic objectives of National Youth Strategies, OECD and selected countries — 33
Figure 2.3. When youth were involved in strategy design, they were more satisfied with results — 40
Figure 2.4. Monitoring and evaluation of National Youth Strategies, OECD and selected countries — 43
Figure 2.5. Thematic focus of National Youth Strategies, OECD and selected countries — 45
Figure 3.1. Organisational Chart of the Ministry of Youth, Jordan, 2021 — 54
Figure 3.2. Composition of the workforce of Ministry of Youth by job category, 2017-20 — 56
Figure 3.3. Budget allocation by the Ministry of Youth, Jordan, 2017-20 — 59
Figure 3.4. Capital expenditures by the Ministry of Youth differ significantly across governorates in Jordan, 2020 — 60
Figure 3.5. Allocation of current expenditures by the Ministry of Youth in 2017-20 — 61
Figure 4.1. Youth trust the armed forces and the police more than political institutions in Jordan — 74
Figure 4.2. A majority of youth in Jordan is not interested in politics at all, comparison across the MENA region — 78
Figure 4.3. Youth in Jordan remains under-represented in parliament, comparison across MENA region — 82
Figure 4.4. Youth official volunteering in Jordan remains limited, comparison across MENA region — 88
Figure 5.1. Minimum age requirements in Jordan compared to OECD average, 2021 — 100
Figure 5.2. Minimum age requirements in political life across selected MENA economies, 2020 — 103

Boxes

Box 2.1. Age-disaggregated evidence in Sweden — 39
Box 2.2. Participatory approaches to youth policy in selected OECD countries — 41
Box 2.3. Mechanisms to monitor and evaluate youth policy and programmes in OECD countries — 44
Box 3.1. Graduate programmes: Attracting and developing young talent in the public administration — 57
Box 3.2. Examples of horizontal co-ordination mechanisms for youth policy — 62
Box 3.3. Youth checks in OECD countries — 65
Box 3.4. How to involve youth in public budgeting? — 66
Box 4.1. Learning and practicing democratic governance — 80
Box 4.2. Developing young talent in the civil service — 81
Box 4.3. Participatory budgeting can help bring young people in — 86
Box 4.4. Structured dialogue between youth and municipalities — 87
Box 4.5. Promoting youth volunteering — 89
Box 5.1. Examples of national youth laws — 98

Follow OECD Publications on:

http://twitter.com/OECD_Pubs

http://www.facebook.com/OECDPublications

http://www.linkedin.com/groups/OECD-Publications-4645871

http://www.youtube.com/oecdilibrary

http://www.oecd.org/oecddirect/

Acronyms and abbreviations

APS	Australian Public Service
ATI	Access to Information
CBO	Community-Based Organisation
CoG	Centre of Government
CRC	United Nations Convention on the Rights of the Child
CSB	Civil Service Bureau
CSO	Civil Society Organisation
EYC	Emirates Youth Council
EU	European Union
IEC	Independent Election Commission
ILO	International Labour Organisation
IFES	International Foundation for Electoral Systems
IPU	Inter-Parliamentary Union
IT	Information Technology
JOD	Jordanian Dinar
JSOP	Jordan School of Politics
KG	kindergarten
KPI	Key Performance Indicator
M&E	Monitoring and Evaluation
MoU	Memorandum of Understanding
MP	Member of Parliament
MENA	Middle East and North Africa
MoPIC	Ministry of Planning and International Cooperation
MoY	Ministry of Youth (in Jordan)
MUCF	Swedish Agency for Youth and Civil Society
NEET	Not in Education, Employment or Training
NGOs	Non-Governmental Organisations
NYS	National Youth Strategy
OECD	Organisation for Economic Cooperation and Development
OGP	Open Government Partnership
PISA	OECD's Programme for International Student Assessment
SWOT	(Analysis of) Strengths, Weaknesses, Opportunities and Threats
TVET	Technical and Vocational Education and Training
UN	United Nations
UNDP	United Nations Development Programme
UNESCO	United Nations Educational, Scientific and Cultural Organisation
UNESCWA	United Nations Economic and Social Commission for Western Asia
UNFPA	United Nations Population Fund
UNHCR	United Nations High Commissioner for Refugees
UNICEF	United Nations International Children's Emergency Fund
USAID	United States Agency for International Development
USD	United States Dollar

VE	Vocational Education
WHO	World Health Organization

Codes for OECD countries

AUS Australia	ESP Spain	JPN Japan	PRT Portugal
AUT Austria	EST Estonia	KOR Korea	SVK Slovak Republic
BEL Belgium	FIN Finland	LTU Lithuania	SVN Slovenia
CAN Canada	FRA France	LUX Luxembourg	SWE Sweden
CHE Switzerland	GBR United Kingdom	LVA Latvia	TUR Turkey
CHL Chile	GRC Greece	MEX Mexico	USA United States
CZE Czech Republic	HUN Hungary	NLD Netherlands	
COL Colombia	IRL Ireland	NOR Norway	
CRI Costa Rica	ISL Iceland	NZL New Zealand	
DEU Germany	ISR Israel	OECD OECD average	
DNK Denmark	ITA Italy	POL Poland	

Codes for MENA economies

ALG Algeria	KWT Kuwait	OMN Oman	TUN Tunisia
BHR Bahrain	LBN Lebanon	PA Palestinian Authority	UAE United Arab Emirates
DJI Djibouti	LBY Libya	QAT Qatar	YEM Yemen
EGY Egypt	MRT Mauritania	KSA Saudi Arabia	
IRQ Iraq	MENA MENA average	SYR Syria	
JOR Jordan	MOR Morocco		

Executive Summary

Youth aged 12-30 make up 36% of Jordan's population. Unemployment levels among 15-24 year-olds, exacerbated by the COVID-19 crisis, reached 50% in the fourth quarter of 2020, up from an already high level of 37% in 2019 (World Bank, 2021[1]). The crisis has disrupted youth's access to public services and their trajectory toward decent jobs, financial independence and other milestones of adulthood.

Young people in Jordan have demonstrated resilience and solidarity in mitigating the crisis by supporting vulnerable groups. The needs of young people should be reflected in response and recovery measures to support their transition to an autonomous life, limit long-term costs and prevent a deterioration of trust in public institutions.

The report assesses the governance arrangements established by the Ministry of Youth (MoY) in Jordan to empower youth and build trust, covering four main dimensions:

- Designing, implementing and tracking progress of Jordan's National Youth Strategy 2019-25.
- Building administrative capacity within the MoY to deliver youth-responsive policies, programmes and services.
- Creating a legal and institutional environment to encourage youth participation in public life and young people's representation in state institutions.
- Reviewing legal frameworks to balance considerations of protecting and empowering youth and providing inclusive access to public services and participation.

A joint vision for youth in Jordan: The National Youth Strategy 2019-25

Jordan is one of only four MENA governments with an operational National Youth Strategy in place. While the strategy is backed by high-level political commitment, there are opportunities to strengthen its governance arrangements and overcome the "implementation challenge." To strengthen feedback loops with youth, in particular vulnerable ones, the Ministry could invest in its financial and human resources, clarify the allocation of responsibilities across stakeholders, and develop effective mechanisms for monitoring, evaluation and multi-stakeholder coordination.

To support the implementation of the National Youth Strategy 2019-25, the Ministry of Youth could consider:

- **Building a system of data collection and storage**, including at the subnational level, and setting clear quality standards for submitting evidence from governmental and non-governmental partners to monitor and evaluate the implementation of MoY's strategic objectives.
- **Collecting age-disaggregated data systematically across all relevant policy areas** in combination with other identity factors in partnership with the Department of Statistics, universities or the private sector.

- **Creating a mechanism for young people and youth-led organisations to support the implementation** of the strategy as well as Jordan's response and recovery plans to mitigate the COVID-19 crisis, creating adequate organisational and technical support.
- **Creating a monitoring and evaluation unit** and building capacities among MoY employees to identify key performance indicators, monitor implementation and evaluate outputs, outcomes and impact of the strategy.
- **Fully operationalising the Steering Committee and creating a technical committee** in order to develop implementation plans, identify funding requirements and clarify monitoring and evaluation duties for all governmental and non-governmental partners.

Building administrative capacity to deliver for youth in Jordan

There is a need to provide targeted training opportunities for MoY's employees and for its staff working in the youth centres, in particular in policy making, youth programming, monitoring and evaluation. While 41% of the ministry's budget is allocated to "youth affairs", only 16% of these resources cover expenditures not related to facilities. Stronger administrative capacity at the local level would enable its network of Youth Directorates and youth centres to deliver youth-responsive programmes and services.

The government of Jordan could consider:

- **Drafting clear job descriptions for each job category** and reviewing the incentive system for employees, introducing transparent performance measures and a merit-based reward system.
- **Setting up a training programme** to strengthen skills and knowledge in policy and programme design, project management, and monitoring and evaluation.
- **Adopting an evidence-based approach to identify the budget needs** of different youth directorates and youth centres to address geographical disparities and inclusive access for youth.
- **Strengthening institutional mechanisms and capacities for co-ordination** across ministries and with sub-national authorities and non-governmental stakeholders to deliver effective policies and services for young people.
- **Mainstreaming the concerns of youth in policy making and service delivery** by considering to apply governance tools in the rule making and public budgeting process.

Youth participation and representation in public life in Jordan

Fewer than 5 in 10 young people in Jordan trust their government and youth tend to vote in elections less than older citizens. Youth's participation in the policy cycle and representation in state institutions remain limited, with a representation gap of 42 percentage points in parliament. At the same time, young people take part in the public debate through non-institutionalised channels. Jordan's National Youth Strategy 2019-25 recognises the importance of promoting youth engagement, effective citizenship and leadership. A strong relationship between youth and public institutions is crucial for ensuring the effectiveness, legitimacy and resilience of institutions.

The government of Jordan could consider:

- **Strengthening civic and citizenship curricula** in schools and out-of-school programmes to reinforce youth's association with democratic processes.
- **Providing programmes to help talented youth join and thrive in the public sector** workforce and promote inter-generational learning between older and younger employees.

- **Adopting a government-wide policy on youth engagement in policy and strengthening in-person and digital means,** including participatory budgeting programmes, youth councils and youth advisory councils.
- **Ensuring an enabling environment and promoting youth participation in public life**, including by associating the MoY and youth stakeholders more closely with national action plans for the Open Government Partnership.
- **Promoting national youth volunteering programmes** and providing political support, resources, mandates and tools to the Higher Committee for Volunteer Work.

Legal frameworks to empower and protect youth in Jordan

Jordan has made significant efforts to align national laws with international standards in the area of children rights, gender discrimination, education, employment, health, justice and others. However, high minimum age requirements continue to exclude a significant share of youth from participation in public and political life. Citizens need to be 30 years old to run for parliament and 25 for local councils, far exceeding the minimum ages across OECD countries and in most MENA countries. In other areas, such as full-time work and hazardous employment, further efforts are needed to enforce existing laws.

To balance concerns about protecting and empowering young people, the government of Jordan could consider:

- **Clearly defining the responsibilities and mandates** of state and non-state institutions working with and for young people, for instance by amending law No. (78) of 2016 or drafting a national youth law to address fragmentation in the delivery of policies, programmes and services for youth.
- **Conducting a review of minimum-age requirements across public services areas** against international benchmarks to identify barriers for youth to access them.
- **Considering lowering minimum age requirements** for candidates for national and subnational elections in line with recommendations by the Royal Constitutional Review Committee.
- **Enforcing laws identifying minimum age requirements** to protect young men and women from harm, for instance working full-time and in hazardous employment.

1 Assessing the situation of youth in Jordan

With around 36%, young people aged 12-30 years constitute more than one third of the population in Jordan. Their successful engagement in the labour market, public and political life, and society is crucial for their personal well-being and economic prospects and for overall economic growth, social cohesion and trust in government. This chapter sets out the context in which youth in Jordan are coming of age. It will discuss national, regional and global factors shaping the opportunities for young people, assess their current situation and cover trends that are likely to shape their lives and that of future generations.

With around 36%, youth in Jordan constitute more than one third of the population when the age group defined by the Ministry of Youth (12-30 years) is considered. Around six in ten people are under the age of 30 (UNICEF, 2021[1]). Figure 1.1 illustrates the population pyramid for Jordan in 2020 and the projected developments for the next ten years. By 2030, the share of 15-25 year-olds is likely to grow further and may represent the single biggest age group according to projections by the United Nations (UN). As today's youth cohort will grow older, the demographic transition presents a unique opportunity for Jordan but also the need for renewed efforts and investments into their transition to an autonomous life and participation in economic, social and public life.

Figure 1.1. Demographic composition of Jordan by age cohort, 2020 and 2030 (forecast)

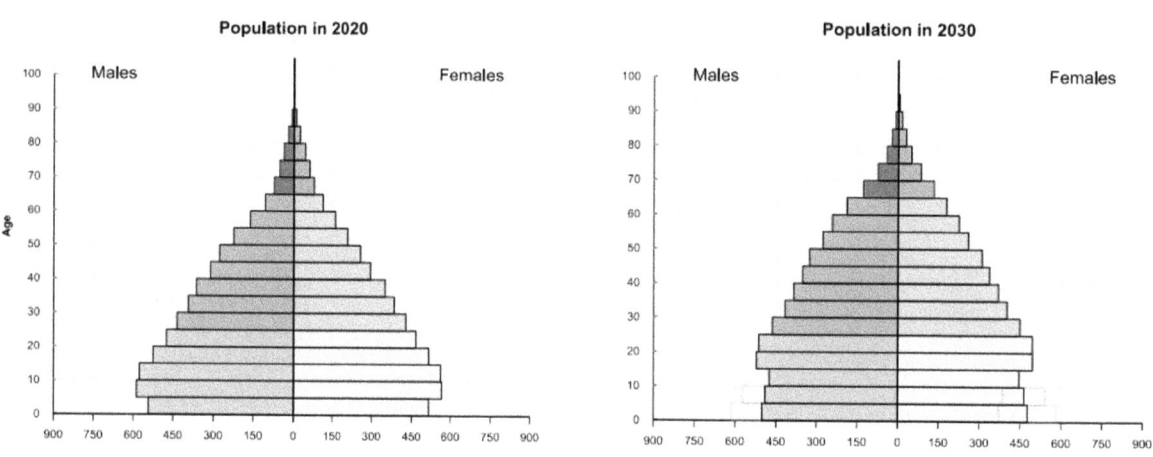

Source: United Nations, Department of Economic and Social Affairs, World Population Prospects, https://population.un.org/wpp/Graphs/1_Demographic%20Profiles/Jordan.pdf.

Youth in Jordan are growing up in a regional context of political and economic instability with significant spill-over effects into the country and significant impacts on its economic development and social cohesion (United Nations, 2017[2]). Since 2010, Gross Domestic Product (GPD) growth has grown by 2.4% annually on average, down from 6.74% in the decade before (World Bank, 2021[3]). Moreover, fiscal space has tightened in recent years with the International Monetary Fund (IMF) reporting risks related to the elevated debt level, fiscal vulnerabilities, and reliance on continued donor financing (IMF, 2019[4]). According to the United Nations High Commissioner for Refugees (UNHCR), Jordan continues to host the highest number of refugees per capita globally with more than 750,000 refugees as of February 2021 (UNHCR, 2021[5]).

The COVID-19 pandemic and its social and economic implications have exacerbated inequalities and the challenges faced by young people, in particular vulnerable groups. School closures, curfews and disrupted access to education have increased inequalities in the access to education. According to the OECD Programme for International Student Assessment (PISA), around 16% of students in Jordan lacked internet access and one third of 15-year-olds did not have a computer for schoolwork in 2018 (OECD, 2021[6]). Youth unemployment levels reached 50% in the fourth quarter of 2020 due to the COVID-19 pandemic, compared to 24.7% among the total population (World Bank, 2021[7]). The COVID-19 crisis has pushed young people further into informal and more precarious jobs with significant impacts on their disposable income and financial independence. It has also put them on a more volatile trajectory in achieving other important milestones of adulthood.

With the closure of youth centres and youth clubs due to sanitary reasons, spaces for social interaction and non-formal learning largely shifted to online platforms. This has raised new concerns about the exclusion of vulnerable groups from online spaces but also the risk of increased exposure to disinformation via social media. In parallel, young people have shown resilience, solidarity with older age cohorts, and agency in mitigating the crisis by supporting vulnerable groups in society, thus fostering social cohesion.

Beyond the impact of COVID-19, other national and global transformations are changing the world in which youth in Jordan are growing up, most notably the fast pace of digitalisation, the future of work, and climate change. In this context, a future-oriented approach to youth policy making and programming is critical to harness new opportunities while mitigating new risks that impact on the wellbeing and resilience of youth.

This chapter sets out the context in which youth in Jordan are coming of age. It will discuss national, regional and global factors shaping young people's opportunities, analyse key indicators to assess the situation of youth and cover some of trends that are likely to shape the lives of today's youth and future generations in the years to come.

National trends driving the perception of government

Improving the situation for youth has long been on the political agenda in Jordan. In 2000, King Abdullah II referred to the young generation as the "greatest asset and hope for the future" and the need to "tap into our young people's intellectual, creative, and reproductive potential in order for Jordan to keep up with new developments in global scientific, economic and social factors" (OECD, 2018[8]). Subsequent discussion papers issued by King Abdullah II have reiterated the need for empowering youth by developing the state administration and enhancing the rule of law (UNESCO, 2017[9]).

The transformation of the Higher Council for Youth into the Ministry of Youth in 2016 marked an important milestone in elevating youth affairs at the government level. In 2019, Jordan launched the National Strategy for Youth 2019-2025. Coordinated by the Ministry of Youth, the adoption of a cross-sectional strategy dedicated to the concerns of young people makes Jordan one of two countries across the MENA region with an operational strategy in place. Jordan was also the first country in the MENA region to adopt a multi-annual youth strategy for the years 2005-2009 to unify and better coordinate the various initiatives targeting youth.

Despite these notable achievements, young people in Jordan continue to face significant challenges in their transition to an autonomous life. The Arab Barometer data (Figure 1.2) shows that, even prior to the COVID-19 crisis, a large majority of the population sees the economic situation as the country's biggest challenge (71%), followed by corruption (17%) (Arab Barometer, 2019[10]).

Figure 1.2. Main concerns raised by survey respondents in Jordan, 2019

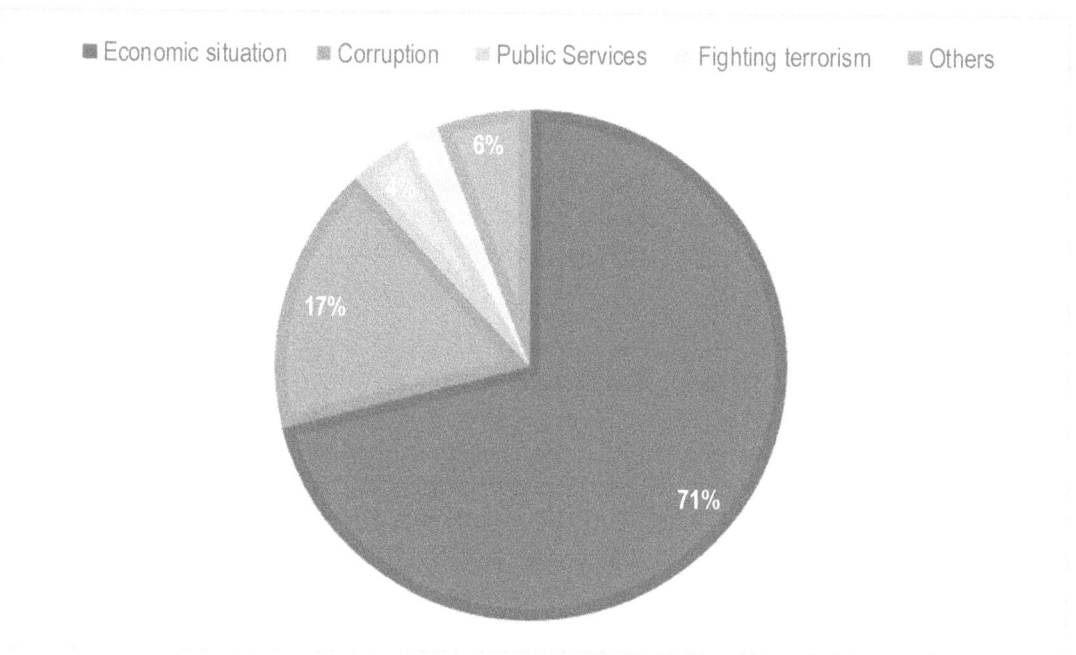

Note: The figure shows the replies of Jordanians to the question: What is the most important challenge facing your country today?
Source: (Arab Barometer, 2019[10])

Over the past decade, satisfaction with the economic situation has declined significantly. While 55% rated the economic situation as good or very good in 2006, only 23% expressed satisfaction with the state of the economy in 2018. Satisfaction rates have dropped most significantly since 2016 (by 23 percentage points from 46% to 23%) (Figure 1.3). Some of the factors contributing to the sharp decline include the austerity measures adopted by Jordan; the refugee crisis accompanied by the decline in global refugee aid1; and the decline in foreign aid. In turn, a third of the respondents were optimistic that the economic situation will improve in the near future as of 2018 (Arab Barometer, 2019[10]).

Figure 1.3. How respondents perceive the economic situation and corruption in Jordan, 2006-2018

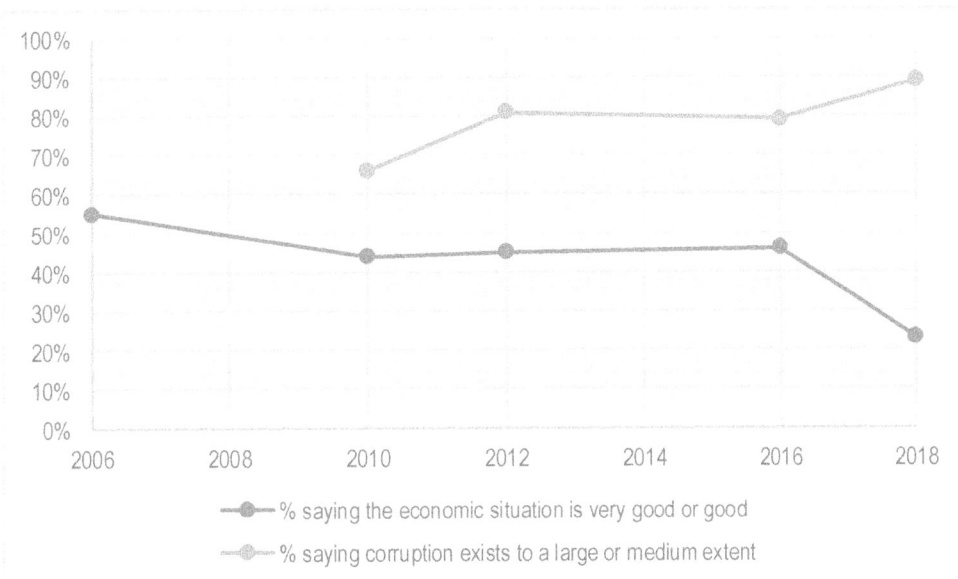

Note: The figure shows the share of respondents saying the current economy is "very good" or "good" (How would you evaluate the current economic situation in your country?) and the share of respondents saying corruption exists to a "large" or "medium" extent (To what extent do you think that there is corruption within the national state agencies and institutions in your country?).
Source: (Arab Barometer, 2019[10])

Corruption is the second biggest challenge as per the perception of the respondents to the Arab Barometer. 89% say that corruption exists to a "large" or "medium" extent in state institutions and agencies, up by more than 30 percentage points from 66% in 2010 (Figure 3) (Arab Barometer, 2019[10]). According to the Corruption Perceptions Index by Transparency International, Jordan scored 49 points in 2021, which places it 60th globally out of 180 countries and 5th in the MENA region. Jordan's performance in the Index has deteriorated between 2005 and 2011 (from a high of 57 points to 45 points) and recovered gradually before effectively stagnating around current levels since 2016 (Figure 1.4) (Economics, 2020[11])[2].

Figure 1.4. Jordan Corruption Index, 2000-2020

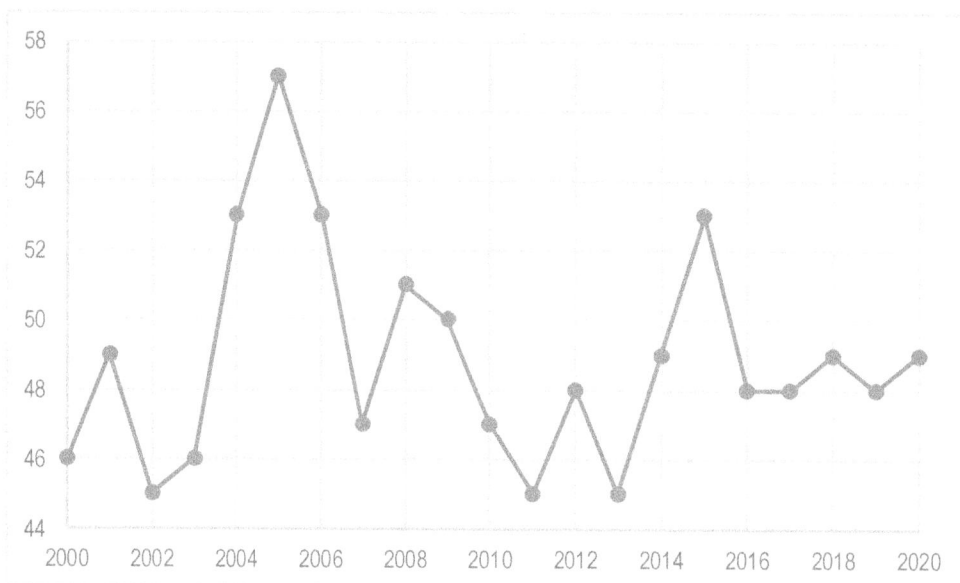

Note: The figure shows the results of the Corruption Perceptions Index for Jordan. The score indicates the perceived level of public sector corruption on a scale of 0 (highly corrupt) to 100 (very clean).
Source: (Economics, 2020[11])

Linked to the dissatisfaction of Jordanians with available economic opportunities and perception of corruption, considerations to emigrate from Jordan have increased in recent years. 45% of survey respondents confirmed that they have been thinking about emigrating from Jordan as of 2018, up from 22% in 2016 (Figure 1.5). Considerations to emigrate are particularly pronounced among educated youth who point to economic considerations as the main reason (83%)[3]. Youth (18-29 years) were significantly more likely to consider emigrating than older age cohorts: Whereas this was considered by 59% of 18-29 year-old, the share drops to 46% for the 30-39 year-old. In contrast, 31% of the 50-59 age cohort and only 16% the respondents aged 60 and older considered emigrating (Arab Barometer, 2019[10]).

Figure 1.5. Share of youth in Jordan considering to emigrate, 2006-2018

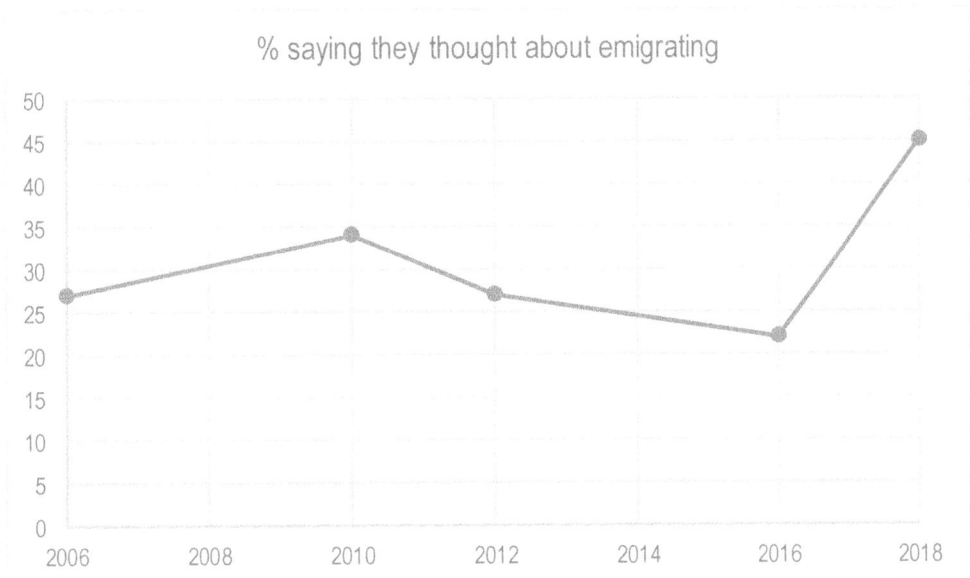

Note: The figure shows the replies of young Jordanians to the question: Have you ever thought about emigrating from Jordan?
Source: (Arab Barometer, 2019[10])

Access of youth to public services and participation in public life

This section will discuss the situation of young people in Jordan in the context of the broader social, economic and political context and national and regional developments. It must be noted that youth are not a homogenous group. Although they might face common social, economic and political experiences given the same period in which they transition from childhood to adulthood, their individual backgrounds, experiences and aspirations are highly diverse. It is therefore important to discuss challenges in people's access to public services and their trust in government not only by age but to complement it with an analysis of other identity factors such as gender and socio-economic background to identify potential vulnerables of specific groups of youth.

Employment: More than one in three youth in Jordan is unemployed

Jordan has one of the highest youth unemployment rates in the MENA region, in particular among young women. Youth unemployment levels in Jordan were never below 25% in the past three decades (OECD, 2018[8]) and has increased to 50% in the fourth quarter of 2020 due to the COVID-19 pandemic, up from an already high share of 37% in 2019 (51% for young women) (World Bank, 2021[7]).

Unemployment among youth is particularly pronounced among well educated youth. For instance, 26% of male holders of a bachelor or higher degree and 77% of female students with a bachelor or higher degree were unemployed in 2018 (Ministry of Education, 2018[12]). Similarly, the rate of young NEET (not in employment, education or training) is significantly higher for young women than young men. In 2019, 44% young women were NEETs in Jordan compared to 29% of young men (Figure 1.6) (World Bank, 2019[13]) (World Bank, 2019[14]).

Figure 1.6. Share of youth not in education, employment or training, Jordan, (2017-2019)

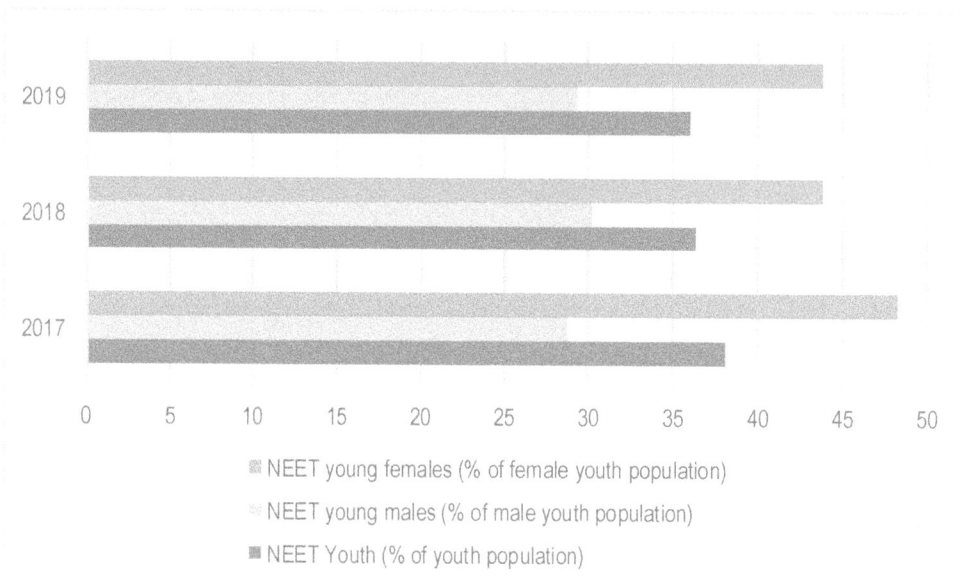

Note: the figure shows the share of NEET youth as total (% of youth population), the share of NEET young males (% of male youth population) and the share of NEET young females (% of female youth population).
Source: (World Bank, 2019[15]).

According to the results of the Arab Barometer (2019), 85% of youth in Jordan are dissatisfied with the performance of government to create employment opportunities (Arab Barometer, 2019[16]). The persistence of high levels of youth unemployment has deep structural roots. Among them, the private sector has not generated enough jobs to absorb young job seekers. Over the past decade, the share of private sector employment relative to employment in the public sector even decreased further (ILO, 2013[17]). Moreover, the public sector is a privileged place to work for many graduates due to the perception of higher job security, shorter working hours, and favourable working conditions (e.g. flexible working hours) despite higher salary prospects in the private sector (USAID, 2015[18]).

There is also a mismatch between the skills tought in school and university and the expertise in demand in the labour market (Arab Barometer, 2019[16]). An assessment by the United States Agency for International Development (USAID) flags that private-sector employers often require extensive trainings and work experience and companies are therefore more reluctant to hire graduates (USAID, 2015[18]). According to a study conducted by the United Nations Development Programme (UNDP), technical know-how, performance under pressure, knowledge and use of new models of machinery, work ethic, and interpersonal skills were among the main challenges raised by private sector representatives (UNDP, 2014[19]). This is acknowledged by self-assessments among students who have been pointing to a "lack of problem-solving, critical thinking and technical skills" (USAID, 2015[18]).

In the absence of decent jobs, a significant share of youth is employed in the informal sector. Young jobseekers often accept informal jobs that do not match their qualification and generate low income, which delays their path to an autonomous life and to achieving what are considered important milestones of adulthood, such as marriage (USAID, 2015[18]). In 2015, 38% of young workers (below 30 years old) were employed in the informal sector, half of whom had higher qualifications than their current occupation. Moreover, 60% in this category received below-average wages (OECD, 2018[8]).

High youth unemployment rates are also linked to the prevalence of Wasta in the Jordanian society[4]. An assessment by USAID finds that 94% of youth in Jordan believe that connections and networks play a more important role in securing employment and getting a job than education and academic performance (Arab Barometer, 2019[16]) (USAID, 2015[18]).

Education: Progress towards gender parity but enrollment rates are on the decline

Jordan has made significant progress in providing access to education. For instance, literacy rates among youth (aged 15-24 years) reached 99% (Statista, 2021[20]), outnumbering the average of 90% across the MENA region in 2019 (UNESCO, 2021[21]) (World Bank, 2019[22]). Jordan also made considerable progress in achieving gender parity in education as illustrated by equal literacy rates and enrolment rates for primary education among young men and women (Statista, 2021[20]). As of 2018, 81% of youth (82% of young men and 80% of young women) were enrolled in primary education, up from 78% in 2011 (World Bank, 2020[23]). Moreover, 87% of young men and 90% of young women were enrolled in secondary education (World Bank, 2020[23]).

However, enrollment rates for primary education of 81% figure below the average of MENA region (94%) and OECD countries (97%). Enrollment rates in secondary education decreased from 77% in 2011 to 63% in 2018 (75% in MENA), similarly, they decreased from 37% in 2011 to 34% in tertiary education (41% in MENA) over the same period (World Bank, n.d.[24]). Challenges in the education sector also relate to the shortage of education staff. In the 2018 edition of the OECD's Programme for International Student Assessment (PISA), school principals reported having one of the largest shortage of education staff among countries participating in the assessment.

In line with patterns across OECD countries, social and economic inequalities contribute to unequal access to schools and learning opportunities in Jordan, which results in unequal learning outcomes and performance. For instance, the shortage of education staff is more pronounced in disadvantaged schools[5]. 47% of students enrolled in a disadvantaged school (compared to 34% in OECD countries) and 30% of students enrolled in an advantaged school (compared to 18% in OECD countries) attend a school whose principal reported that the capacity of the school to provide instructions is hindered at least to "some extent" by a lack of teaching staff (OECD, 2018[25]). The findings also demonstrate that students from socio-economically disadvantaged backgrounds hold lower ambitions related to their academic achievements than more advantaged students even when the high-achievers in both groups are considered.[6]

To address the mismatch of skills in the labour market, Jordan's Education Strategic Plan (2018-2022) stresses the importance of developing an advanced system of Technical and Vocational Education and Training (TVET) to better meet the needs of the labour market. However, TVET continues to be perceived negatively by students and families as it is considered a "second-class route for low performing students" (Ministry of Education, 2018[12]). In response, the Ministry of Education intends to make this sector more attractive for students by providing Vocational Education to secondary schools (grades 11-12)[7] in areas such as industry, agriculture, hotel and tourism, and household production. While around 43% of Vocational Education (VE) students are women, data shows that gender biases and stereotypes persist. For instance, whereas the majority of young men are enrolled in the industrial, hotel, tourism and agricultural sectors, almost 98% of all students enrolled in household production are young women. VE trainings in industry, agriculture, hotel and tourism sector often take place in boys' schools, which exclude or discourage female students from attending the same classes. Social norms continue to exert a strong influence on students' choices as many females consider home-based activities "appropriate" while acknowledging that such activities do not prepare them adequately for the job market (USAID, 2015[18]).

Child labour, caused by poverty and adult unemployment, further restricts young people's access to education. According to the International Labour Organisation (ILO), around 70,000 children, aged 5-17, were exposed to child labour in 2018, 62,500 of which are boys and 7,500 are girls (Ministry of Education, 2018[12]). Data from the Ministry of Labour in 2010 shows that 40% of the fathers of children exposed to child labour are unemployed and 70% live in families that are living below the extreme poverty line

(UNICEF, 2014[26]). More recent data suggests that child poverty is on the rise, reaching 20% in 2018 (The Jordan Times, 2018[27]).

Health: Reckless driving, smoking, obesity and unequal access to services are key risks

Important health indicators have improved in Jordan over recent decades while important challenges prevail. For instance, infant mortality rate declined from 18 per 1000 births in 2010 to 14 in 2018, which is below the average of 18 in the MENA region (World Bank Data, 2019[28]). With 8% of GDP, Jordan allocated a higher share of its GDP to public health expenditures than the MENA region (5.7%) but less than OECD countries (12.6%) in 2017 (World Bank Data, 2020[29]). In 2019, 63% of survey respondents to the Arab Barometer from Jordan expressed satisfaction with the healthcare system. This presents a significant decline from a share of 86% in 2016 (Arab Barometer, 2019[10]). At the policy level, Jordan Vision 2025 acknowledges the importance of establishing youth-friendly health care centres to treat mental health issues and drug abuse among the young generation (UNESCO and OECD, 2020[30]).

Health risks among young people in Jordan are linked to high-risk behaviour, such as the prevalence of smoking, unhealty nutrition, and reckless traffic behaviour. As indicated by the 2019 annual report on traffic accidences of the Jordanian Public Security Directorate, young drivers (below 33 years) have the highest rates of road traffic accidents, compared to older age groups (Public Security Directorate, 2019[31]). Likewise, the rate of smoking among adolescents (aged 13-15) increased up to 24% in 2014 (34% among young men and 14% among young women). This also concerns the consumption of Argileh among youth, which, at odds with scientific evidence, is often considered less harmful and addictive by adolescents[8]. 12% of young persons aged 15-18 is obese (OECD, 2018[8]). According to a study conducted by World Health Organization (WHO) in the Governorate of Irbid, obesity among adolescents aged 13-16 years was significantly higher among female students, students who lived in urban areas and those with working parents (WHO, 2010[32]). In addition, as reported by the Ministry of Health in 2011, diabetes represents a major health problem. In 2016, more than a third of the adult population (18 years and above) was affected by it (Jordan Times, 2019[33]).

Young women, youth in rural areas, and youth with disabilities face specific challenges in their access to health services and health facilities (OECD, 2018[8]). For instance, sexual and reproductive health awareness is limited among youth in Jordan, especially among young women. According to a study conducted by WHO on contraceptive methods, there is still a high use of traditional contraceptive methods, which increases the risk of an undesired pregnancy (WHO, 2018[34]).

Youth participation in public and political life in Jordan

Over the past decade, Jordan has undertaken important reform efforts to strengthen more open, participatory and inclusive policymaking. In 2012, Jordan was the first Arab country to join the Open Government Partnership (OGP) and, by 2018, it launched its 4th National Action Plan for 2018-20 (Open Government Partnership, 2019[35]). The current Action Plan is the first to acknowledge that youth institutions shall be included in the national dialogue (Chapter 4). Moreover, Jordan's National Youth Strategy 2019-25 highlights the need to "promote youth work and the development of young people in an educational, skilful and valuable way, enabling them to innovate, create, produce and participate in political life and public affairs" (Ministry of Youth in Jordan, 2019[36]) (Chapter 2). Internationally, led by Crown Prince Hussein bin Abdullah, Jordan has been one of the driving countries to adopt UN Security Council Resolution 2250 on Youth, Peace and Security, which recognises the role of youth in promoting and maintaining international peace (UNESCO, 2017[9]).

At national level, Jordan has engaged in decentralisation reform with the aim to reduce territorial disparities and provide new opportunities for citizens to participate in the identification of local needs and priorities. In 2017, the Ministry of Youth provided youth directors, who oversee youth-related programmes and the work of youth centres across the governorates, with greater administrative and financial autonomy and facilitated approval procedures (Chapter 3). However, access of youth from remote areas to government services and programmes remains unequal and demonstrates the need for continuous efforts to build administrative capacity, especially at the subnational level (OECD, 2017[37]). Other important changes to encourage (young people's) participation in political life concern the Election Law in 2016, among others (Chapter 4).

Despite these initiatives, structural barriers for young people to participate in public and political life remain to be addressed. Youth participation in national and subnational elections remains low. Voters under 30 years of age represented 38% of the people who participated in the 2020 parliamentary elections in Jordan (Rased, 2020[38]). In 2016, 35% of those who voted were below the age of 30. 41% of surveyed people aged 18-29 reported having voted in the 2016 parliamentary election, while 55% of people aged above 30 did so (European Union Election Observation Mission, 2016[39]). Moreover, trust among youth in political institutions and leaders is low, especially in parliament (23%) and political parties (12%) (OECD, 2018[8]). As Chapter 4 will discuss in detail, young people's dissatisfaction in political institutions has been on the rise since 2010 (Arab Barometer, 2019[10]). Less than 3% of youth in Jordan are members of a charitable society and organised in a youth, cultural or sports organisation as of 2013 (OECD, 2018[40]). To address this challenge, Jordan Vision 2025 acknowledges the importance of encouraging young people to volunteer and to create a National Coordinating Volunteer Council (UNESCO, 2017[9]).

The enactment of the Defence Law to enforce the COVID-19 lockdown measures prompted a debate about a balanced approach to protecting public health while ensuring civic rights and liberties to create an enabling environment for youth to participate in public life (Freedom House, 2020[41]) (Chapter 4).

Outline of the report

The report is divided into four thematic chapters to assess the capacities of the government of Jordan to deliver policies and services that are responsive to the needs of youth.

A joint vision for youth in Jordan: The National Youth Strategy 2019-25

This Chapter will analyse the governance arrangements put in place to design, steer, coordinate and track progress in the implementation of Jordan's National Youth Strategy (NYS) 2019-25. For this purpose, it will benchmark the arrangements in place against the eight principles of good governance as set out in the OECD Assessment Framework of National Youth Strategies to identify strengths and opportunities to build up further administrative capacity and partnerships.

It will provide comparative evidence from across MENA and OECD countries to translate the commitments of national integrated youth strategies into tangible improvements in the lives of youth.

Building administrative capacity to deliver for youth in Jordan

This Chapter examines the formal organisation of youth affairs in Jordan with a focus on the administrative capacity within the Ministry of Youth, with a focus on human and financial resources. It will analyse the coordination mechanisms established horizontally (across ministerial departments) and vertically (across the different levels of government) to translate its strategic objectives into programmes and activities across Jordan's 12 governorates and explore the tools used to mainstram youth's concerns in programming.

It will complement the analysis with good practice examples from across MENA and OECD countries to build administrative capacity in the lead government entity in charge of youth affairs.

Rebuilding youth relationship with Jordan's public institutions

This chapter discusses how the government of Jordan can strengthen youth participation and representation in public life. Youth trust in public institutions and representation in decision-making remain limited in Jordan, with the risk of young people disassociating from public and political life. Governance arrangements, laws, policies and institutions can be leveraged to promote a stronger relationship between youth and public institutions.

Based on an assessment of the current situation, ongoing reform initiatives and good practices from MENA and OECD countries, this chapter provides policy recommendations to empower youth in public life.

Legal frameworks to empower and protect youth in Jordan

This chapter addresses to what extent key legal frameworks are responsive to young people's needs and provide opportunities for them to participate in public and political life. It analyses minimum age criteria set up to vote and run in elections and those that determine access to employment, education, health, justice and other services that are critical for the transition of youth to an autonomous life.

The Chapter will benchmark the current criteria in place against the thresholds set across MENA and OECD countries in a constant effort of balancing concerns about protecting and empowering young men and women.

References

Arab Barometer (2019), *Jordan Country Report*, https://www.arabbarometer.org/wp-content/uploads/ABV_Jordan_Report_Public-Opinion-2019.pdf. [10]

Arab Barometer (2019), *Youth Report, Public Opinion Middle East and North Africa,*, https://www.arabbarometer.org/wp-content/uploads/ABV_Youth_Report_Public-Opinion_Middle-East-North-Africa_2019-1.pdf. [16]

Economics, T. (2020), *Jordan Corruption Index*, https://tradingeconomics.com/jordan/corruption-index. [11]

European Union Election Observation Mission (2016), *The Hashemite Kingdom of Jordan: Parliamentary Election 20 September 2016*, https://www.europarl.europa.eu/cmsdata/212604/Jordan_parliamentary-elections_20-September-2016_EU-EOM-report.pdf (accessed on 6 May 2021). [39]

Freedom House (2020), , https://www.ecoi.net/en/document/2046522.html. [41]

ILO (2013), *Decent work country profile: Hashemite Kingdom of Jordan*, https://www.ilo.org/wcmsp5/groups/public/---dgreports/---integration/documents/publication/wcms_232764.pdf. [17]

IMF (2019), *IMF Jordan Country Report No. 19/127*, http://file:///C:/Users/Hosny_M/Downloads/1JOREA2019001%20(1).pdf. [4]

Jordan Times (2019), *'Obesity in Jordan rises by 300,000 in four years'*, https://jordantimes.com/news/local/obesity-jordan-rises-300000-four-years. [33]

Ministry of Education, J. (2018), *Education Strategic Plan*, http://www.unesco.org/new/fileadmin/MULTIMEDIA/FIELD/Amman/pdf/ESP_English.pdf. [12]

Ministry of Youth in Jordan (2019), *National Youth Strategy 2019-2025*, http://moy.gov.jo/sites/default/files/jordan_national_youth_strategy_2019-2025_english_compressed_1.pdf (accessed on 12 May 2021). [36]

OECD (2021), *PISA*, https://www.oecd.org/pisa/. [6]

OECD (2018), *The Programme for International Student Assessment (PISA) Results for Jordan,*, https://www.oecd.org/pisa/publications/PISA2018_CN_JOR.pdf. [25]

OECD (2018), *Youth Engagement and Empowerment*, https://www.oecd.org/mena/governance/youth-engagement-and-empowerment-report.pdf. [40]

OECD (2018), *Youth Well-being Policy Review in Jordan*, https://www.oecd.org/dev/inclusivesocietiesanddevelopment/Youth_well_being_policy_review_Jordan.pdf. [8]

OECD (2017), *OECD Open Government Review in Jordan*, https://www.oecd.org/mena/governance/Jordan-Highlights-2017.pdf. [37]

Open Government Partnership (2019), *Jordan Action Plan 2018-2020*, https://www.opengovpartnership.org/documents/jordan-action-plan-2018-2020/. [35]

Public Security Directorate, J. (2019), *2019 Annual Report on Traffic Accidences in Jordan*, https://www.psd.gov.jo/images/docs/TrafficRep2019.pdf?fbclid=IwAR1ZvII_waPNv5edbwsw1Xn9aaRCSJbr8hKZMV6lRUS7Ph4wddQ-PtfiKZY. [31]

Rased (2020), *Final Report on the Outcomes of Observing the Jordanian Parliamentary Elections 2020*, https://www.rasedjo.com/ar/publications (accessed on 6 May 2021). [38]

Statista (2021), *Jordan: Literacy Rate from 2007 to 2018*, https://www.statista.com/statistics/572748/literacy-rate-in-jordan/. [20]

The Jordan Times (2018), *20% of children in Jordan still suffering from poverty — UNICEF*, https://jordantimes.com/news/local/20-children-jordan-still-suffering-poverty-%E2%80%94-unicef. [27]

UNDP (2014), *Labour Market: The Case of Vocational Training in Jordan,*, https://www.knowledge4all.com/en/210/Publications/Labour-Market--The-Case-of-Vocational-Training-in-Jordan. [19]

UNESCO (2021), *Sustainable Development Goals*, http://data.uis.unesco.org/. [21]

UNESCO (2017), *Assessing the broader youth environment in Jordan*, http://www.unesco.org/new/fileadmin/MULTIMEDIA/FIELD/Amman/pdf/Assessing_broader_youth_environment_JOR.pdf. [9]

UNESCO and OECD (2020), *Assessing the broader youth environment in Jordan*, http://www.unesco.org/new/fileadmin/MULTIMEDIA/FIELD/Amman/pdf/Assessing_broader_youth_environment_JOR.pdf. [30]

UNHCR (2021), *Jordan*, https://reporting.unhcr.org/sites/default/files/Jordan%20country%20factsheet%20-%20February%202021.pdf. [5]

UNICEF (2021), *Youth*, https://www.unicef.org/jordan/youth. [1]

UNICEF (2014), *Jordan, Country Report on Out of School Children*, https://www.unicef.org/mena/sites/unicef.org.mena/files/2019-11/Jordan%20Country%20Report%20on%20OOSC_EN.pdf. [26]

United Nations (2017), *Jordan's Way to Sustainable Development: Review on the Implementation of the 2030 Agenda*, https://sustainabledevelopment.un.org/content/documents/16289Jordan.pdf. [2]

USAID (2015), *Jordan National Youth Assesment*, https://pdf.usaid.gov/pdf_docs/PA00KBZD.pdf. [18]

WHO (2018), *Are users of modern and traditional contraceptive methods in Jordan different?*, http://www.emro.who.int/emhj-volume-24-2018/volume-24-issue-4/are-users-of-modern-and-traditional-contraceptive-methods-in-jordan-different.html. [34]

WHO (2010), *Prevalence of overweight and obesity among adolescents in Irbid governorate, Jordan*,, http://www.emro.who.int/emhj-volume-16-2010/volume-16-issue-6/article-13.html. [32]

World Bank (2021), *GDP growth (annual %) - Jordan, Middle East & North Africa*, https://data.worldbank.org/indicator/NY.GDP.MKTP.KD.ZG?locations=JO-ZQ. [3]

World Bank (2021), *Jordan: The World Bank Group Adapts its Strategy to Support COVID-19 Response, Inclusive and Resilient Recovery, and Continued Reforms*, https://www.worldbank.org/en/news/press-release/2021/05/28/jordan-the-world-bank-group-adapts-its-strategy-to-support-covid-19-response-inclusive-and-resilient-recovery-and-contin. [7]

World Bank (2020), *School enrollment, primary, male (% net) - Jordan*, https://data.worldbank.org/indicator/SE.PRM.NENR.MA?locations=JO. [23]

World Bank (2019), *Literacy rate, youth total (% of people ages 15-24) - Middle East & North Africa, Jordan*, https://data.worldbank.org/indicator/SE.ADT.1524.LT.ZS?locations=ZQ-JO. [22]

World Bank (2019), *Share of youth not in education, employment or training, female (% of female youth population)*, https://data.worldbank.org/indicator/SL.UEM.NEET.FE.ZS. [14]

World Bank (2019), *Share of youth not in education, employment or training, male (% of male youth population)*, https://data.worldbank.org/indicator/SL.UEM.NEET.MA.ZS. [13]

World Bank (2019), *Share of youth not in education, employment or training, total (% of youth population) - Jordan*, https://data.worldbank.org/indicator/SL.UEM.NEET.ZS?locations=JO. [15]

World Bank (n.d.), *School Enrollment, Secondary,*, https://data.worldbank.org/indicator/SE.SEC.NENR?locations=JO. [24]

World Bank Data (2020), *Current health expenditure (% of GDP) - Jordan*, https://data.worldbank.org/indicator/SH.XPD.CHEX.GD.ZS?locations=JO. [29]

World Bank Data, H. (2019), *Mortality rate, infant (per 1,000 live births) - Jordan*, https://data.worldbank.org/indicator/SP.DYN.IMRT.IN?locations=JO. [28]

Notes

[1] According to UNHCR, Jordan continues to host the highest number of refugees per capita globally with 753,282 refugees in February 2021, including 664,414 Syrian refugees, almost 50 percent of whom are adolescents and children (UNHCR, 2021[5]). https://reliefweb.int/report/jordan/unhcr-jordan-factsheet-october-2018; https://www.atlanticcouncil.org/blogs/menasource/factbox-jordan-s-austerity-protests/

[2] A country or territory's score indicates the perceived level of public sector corruption on a scale of 0 (highly corrupt) to 100 (very clean). https://tradingeconomics.com/jordan/corruption-index

[3] More than four in five Jordanians who consider emigrating highlight economic reasons (83 percent), compared to 17 percent for other reasons such as: educational opportunities (4 percent), corruption (2 percent), family reunion (1 percent), and others (9 percent), https://www.arabbarometer.org/wp-content/uploads/ABV_Jordan_Report_Public-Opinion-2019.pdf

[4] Wasta is the practice of favoritism based on family and tribal relations and not on the person's qualifications or expertise.

[5] Socio-economically disadvantaged schools are schools in the bottom 25% of the national distribution of the school-level ESCS index, which is calculated as the average ESCS index among students in a school. Socio-economically advantaged schools are schools in the top 25% of the national distribution of the school-level ESCS index. https://www.educacionyfp.gob.es/dam/jcr:1f3a39fe-505f-44f7-99c8-a676edd42d0d/equity%20in%20education.pdf

[6] Socio-economically disadvantaged students as those whose value on the PISA index of economic, social and cultural status (ESCS) is among the bottom 25% of students within their country or economy. Socio-economically advantaged students as those whose ESCS is among the top 25% of students within their country or economy. https://www.educacionyfp.gob.es/dam/jcr:1f3a39fe-505f-44f7-99c8-a676edd42d0d/equity%20in%20education.pdf

[7] In Jordan, the VE enrolment last for two years (grades 11 and 12). After successfully finishing the tenth grade and taking the General Secondary School Certificate Examination, students can be enrolled in VE. http://www.unesco.org/new/fileadmin/MULTIMEDIA/FIELD/Amman/pdf/ESP_English.pdf

[8] Due to the public misconceptions about tobacco products, many young people do not realise that one hour of argileh consumption equals smoking 100 cigarettes. http://jo.one.un.org/en/press-releases/the-ministry-of-health-and-the-united-nations-in-jordan-call-upon-everyone-to-unite-to-end-tobacco-use/102

2 A joint vision for youth in Jordan: The National Youth Strategy 2019-25

This chapter will analyse the governance arrangements put in place to design, steer, coordinate and track progress in the implementation of Jordan's National Youth Strategy (NYS) 2019-25. For this purpose, it will benchmark the arrangements in place against the eight principles of good governance as set out in the OECD Assessment Framework of National Youth Strategies to identify strengths and opportunities to build up further administrative capacity and partnerships. The chapter will provide comparative evidence from across MENA and OECD countries to translate the commitments of national integrated youth strategies into tangible improvements in the lives of youth.

Jordan is one of four economies along with Kuwait, the Palestinian Authority and the United Arab Emirates in the MENA region with an operational National Youth Strategy (NYS) in place.[1] After its adoption by Cabinet in May 2019, Jordan's National Strategy for Youth 2019-25 was launched in the presence of then Prime Minister Omar Razzaz in July 2019.

The adoption of the Strategy at the highest political level presents a significant step to place young people's concerns more prominently on the political agenda. It formulates the mission to "promote youth work and the development of young people in an educational, skilful and valuable way, enabling them to innovate, create, produce and participate in political life and public affairs" (Ministry of Youth in Jordan, 2019[1]). It also underlines the need to address contemporary challenges and to foster sustainable development by strengthening youth's resilience. Its vision and mission statements are supported by speeches delivered by King Abdullah II and national frameworks, such as Jordan's Vision 2025 and the Renaissance Plan.

The COVID-19 crisis has unveiled the importance of an integrated approach to the delivery of public programmes and services to young people. Youth in Jordan have been hit hard by the social and economic consequences of the crisis (Chapter 1) as existing concerns and vulnerabilities, especially among young people at risk, have risen (e.g. youth living in poor households, school drop-outs, unemployed youth, disabled youth). Indeed, the risk of young people falling into poverty and cut access to income, employment opportunities, access to education and mental and physical health support has been aggravated by the pandemic. The closure of universities, schools, youth centres and other spaces for youth to meet, interact and learn has cut back on social life and connections and risks leaving "scaring" effects on their future careers and earnings, and ultimately pensions. For instance, OECD estimates show that a lost school year can be considered equivalent to a loss of between 7% and 10% of lifetime income (OECD, 2020[2]). To avoid that inequalities at a young age compound over the life circle, governments must create an environment in which young people have access to quality public services. Disruptions in young people's transition to the classical milestones of adulthood also creates significant long-term costs for societies and economies, undermining social cohesion and inclusive growth (OECD, 2020[3]).

This Chapter will not review in detail the programmes covered by the strategy and to what extent they are fit to lift youth on a more positive trajectory after COVID-19. Instead, it will analyse the processes, institutional capacities and engagement formats put in place to help design, implement and monitor and evaluate its strategic objectives. Its ambition is genuinely practical: previous strategies were suspended due to changing political priorities and gaps in the governance arrangements to implement and track progress (Ministry of Youth in Jordan, 2019[1]; OECD, 2018[4]). In support of MoY's ambition to translate its commitments into tangible improvements in the lives of young men and women, the Chapter will identify strengths and opportunities to invest into its administrative capacity to steer, coordinate and build strategic partnerships for this purpose.

It is organised in three sections:

First, it will discuss the benefits of investing into the quality of national integrated youth strategies and introduce the OECD Assessment Framework of National Youth Strategies;

Second, it will benchmark Jordan's National Youth Strategy 2019-25 against the eight principles of good governance as set out in the OECD Assessment Framework and provide comparative evidence from across MENA and OECD countries;

Third, based on the assessment, it will present policy recommendations for the Ministry of Youth and its governmental and non-governmental partners to steer, coordinate, and track progress of the NYS 2019-25 efficiently and effectively.

Investments into national integrated youth strategies pay off

OECD findings demonstrate that investments into the quality of National Youth Strategies pay off with a return. In OECD countries that rank higher in the OECD Assessment Framework for National Youth Strategies, which will be introduced below, young people are more likely to express higher interest in politics (OECD, 2020[3]). OECD data gathered during the COVID-19 pandemic among youth-led organisations also demonstrates that effective, inclusive and transparent governance is an important driver of trust of young people in governments and contributes to the legitimacy of government action (OECD, 2020[5]). Moreover, such strategies can help address the risk of policy fragmentation, mobilise public (and private) resources for youth programming and clarify the mandates of various stakeholders involved. It is important to note that adopting an integrated youth strategy alone, however, is not sufficient and that countries pursuing a more "mainstreamed approach" (i.e. greater responsibility with individual entities without overarching framework) can also deliver positive results if certain conditions are met (i.e. strong co-ordination and monitoring and evaluation frameworks in place).

In 2004, Jordan was the first country in the MENA region to announce a multi-annual strategy focused on young people. However, as will be discussed further below, the results of previous attempts to roll out a whole-of-government youth strategy have remained behind expectations (Milton-Edwards, 2018[6]; OECD, 2016[7]). With the adoption of the NYS 2019-25, Jordan joined Kuwait, Lebanon, Mauritania and the Palestinian Authority among the OECD-surveyed MENA economies. In addition, at least four MENA economies have been in the process of elaborating a strategy, as of May 2021.

Figure 2.1. National Youth Strategies in the MENA region

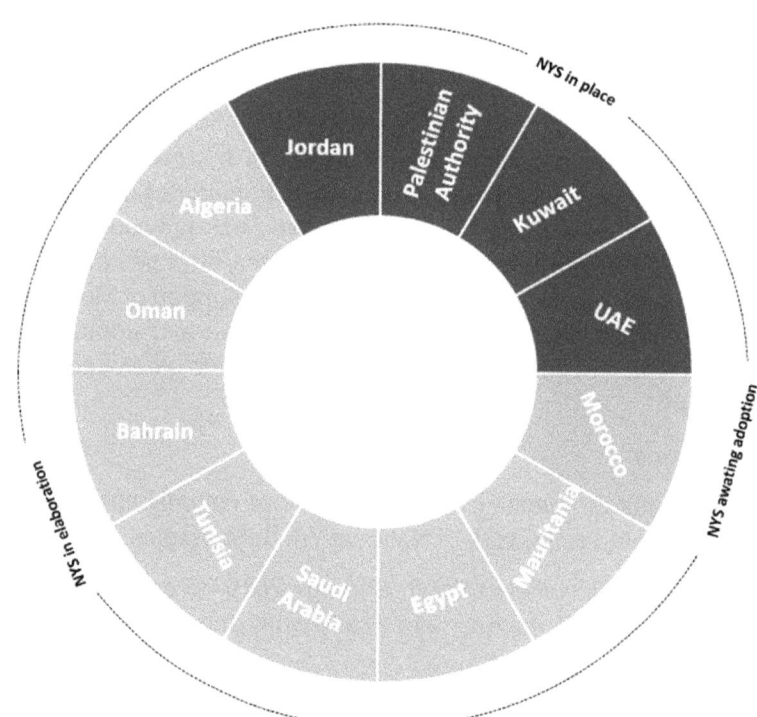

Note: Qatar does not have a National Youth Strategy but its National Development Strategy (2018-2022) on "Cultural Enrichment and Sports Excellence" features a pillar on youth empowerment and sports excellence. Morocco's youth strategy (*Stratégie Nationale Intégrée de la Jeunesse 2015-2030*) is not adopted by Cabinet yet. The status of the Youth Policy in Lebanon, endorsed in 2012, is unclear.
Source: OECD Youth Governance Survey and desk research (updated in May 2021).

Youth policy, programming and service delivery cuts across various ministerial departments and portfolios, levels of government and the mandate of various non-governmental stakeholders. In Jordan, community-based organisations (CBOs) play a critical role at subnational level, often in remote areas, to provide trainings to develop young people's skills and raise awareness for their rights. Moreover, various foundations affiliated to the Royal Court and non-governmental organisations with a broader mandate run important initiatives for youth in areas such as active citizenship, employment training, critical thinking, and access to mental health services and others. While the involvement of a wide range of stakeholders can facilitate expanding access to critical services, such systems must mitigate the risk of fragmentation.

National Integrated Youth Strategies can help overcome fragmented coverage, integrate youth-specific considerations in sectoral policies and allocate clear mandates and mechanisms to ensure co-ordination. Notably, young people (organised and non-organised) are not simply passive recipients of public services but should have an active stake to inform its priorities, identify opportunities for partnerships in the implementation and hold government to account in keeping track of its progress as recognised by Jordan's strategy (Ministry of Youth in Jordan, 2019[1]). In turn, National Youth Strategies can help mobilise public resources for youth programming and serve as important tool to set and communicate the rationale, objectives and expected outcomes for its younger citizens.

Across the OECD, around 76% (25 out of 33) of member countries, for which data is available, have an operational national or federal multi-year youth strategy in place. Results from the OECD Youth Governance Reviews demonstrate that the three top concerns for countries adopting a NYS are to support youth in their transition to adult life (100%), to engage them in the decision-making process (88%) and to integrate their concerns across all relevant policy and service areas (84%) (OECD, 2020[3]). Besides, 64% of government entities in charge of youth affairs point to the importance of strengthening governance tools and mechanisms to deliver policy outcomes that are responsive to young people's demands.

Figure 2.2. Strategic objectives of National Youth Strategies, OECD and selected countries

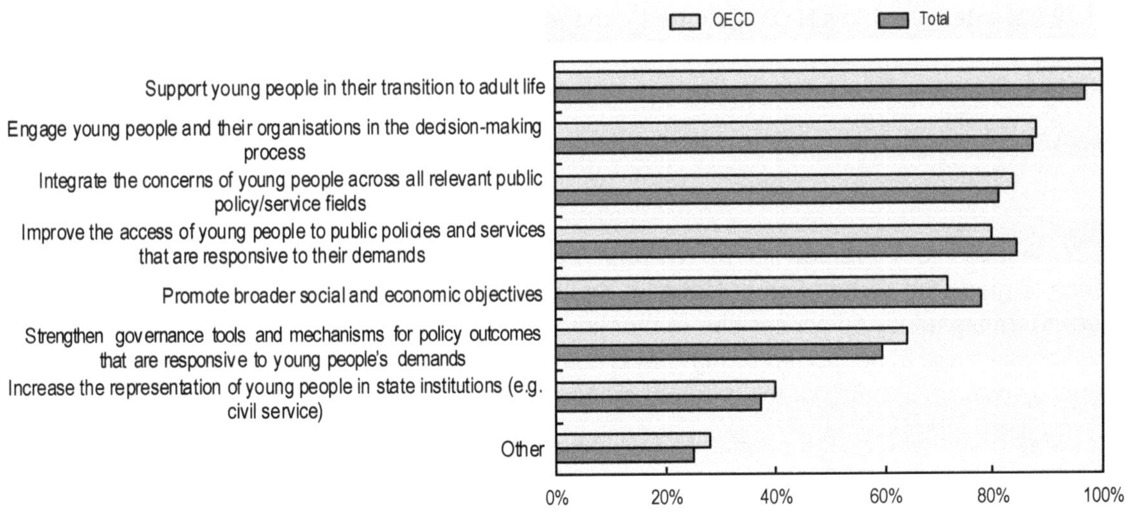

Note: Total refers to 32 countries, which consist of 25 OECD member and 7 non-member countries that have or are elaborating a NYS. OECD refers to 25 countries.
Source: (OECD, 2020[3]).

Whereas the national objective identified by Jordan's National Youth Strategy 2019-25 is focused on "building a generation capable of creativity and innovation with high productivity", it acknowledges also the need for investments into broader governance arrangements (Ministry of Youth in Jordan, 2019[1]). Notably, it calls for MoY's institutional capacities, networking and partnerships, physical infrastructure (e.g. youth centres) and respective human resources (e.g. skills of youth centre staff), and capacity to provide targeted approaches in the work with youth with diverse interests, priorities, age and geographic background. Moreover, youth empowerment and their integration into public life are identified as cross-cutting priorities.

The strategy identifies seven themes, which are further expanded in the form of nine strategic objectives (Table 2.1), each of which is linked to one of the Sustainable Development Goals (i.e. poverty reduction; good health and prosperity; good education; industry, innovation and infrastructure; reducing inequalities; peace, justice and strong institutions; entering into partnerships to achieve objectives).

Table 2.1. NYS 2019-25: Themes and strategic objectives

Themes	Strategic Objectives
Youth, Education and Technology	Developing a safe, supportive and stimulating educational and scientific learning environment by using IT
Youth and Effective Citizenship	Promoting the concepts of culture and citizenship, national identity, and paying attention to the values of belonging, justice and engagement without discrimination
Youth, Engagement and Effective Leadership	Empowering young people in the political, social and economic fields
	Building the capacity of young people and their partners to establish and manage effective initiatives
	Developing youth centres and the infrastructure to provide advanced youth services and to provide friendly spaces
Youth, Pioneering and Economic Engagement	Developing the youth work environment to support creativity, innovation and entrepreneurship to advance social entrepreneurship and non-traditional coping with challenges
Youth, Good Governance and Rule of Law	Promoting the concepts, values and practices of good governance and the rule of law
Youth and Community Security and Peace	Disseminating the culture of tolerance and acceptance of others among the youth, thus promoting social security and peace, and rejecting extremism and violence
Youth, Health and Physical Activity	Raising health awareness among young people and using sound health patterns

Source: (Ministry of Youth in Jordan, 2019[1]).

The next section will introduce the OECD Assessment Framework of National Youth Strategies and discuss to what extent Jordan's NYS is aligned with the eight principles of good governance it builds upon. It will identify the strategy's core strengths and opportunities to reinforce mechanisms, processes and administrative capacities to achieve its strategic objectives.

Reinforcing capacities to steer strategy, coordinate and track progress

The OECD Assessment Framework of National Youth Strategies identifies eight principles of good governance to guide the elaboration of National Youth Strategies: 1) evidence-based, 2) participatory, 3) resourced, 4) transparent and accessible, 5) monitored, evaluated and accountable, 6) cross-sectoral, 7) gender-responsive and 8) supported by high-level political commitment. It provides an integrated approach to guide policy makers throughout the different stages of the youth strategy cycle.

The framework draws on OECD instruments, including the OECD Recommendation on Open Government (OECD, 2017[8]), Gender Equality in Public Life (OECD, 2016[9]), Regulatory Policy and Governance (OECD, 2012[10]), Budgetary Governance (OECD, 2015[11]), Policy Coherence for Sustainable Development (OECD, 2019[12]) and the OECD Policy Framework on Sound Public Governance (OECD, 2019[13]). It also takes into account guidelines prepared at the international level, such as the Lisboa+21 Declaration by the World Conference of Ministers Responsible for Youth 2019, the Baku Commitment to Youth Policies and principles elaborated by international and non-governmental organisations.

Besides the eight core principles, it provides further definitions and explanations to operationalise each and allow for benchmarking or comparing country practices (Table 2.2). Findings from the OECD Youth Governance Surveys demonstrate that positive outcomes in one quality standard are associated with positive outcomes in others, hence suggesting that they are mutually reinforcing. Therefore, they should be pursued by policy makers in tandem.

Table 2.2. OECD Assessment Framework of National Youth Strategies

Principle	Definition and Explanations
Supported by political commitment	Definition: The country's leadership has committed to tackle youth's needs. Explanation: (i) High-level statements outlining youth as government priority; and (ii) "youth" covered in strategic government documents (e.g. national development strategy).
Evidence-based	Definition: all stages of youth policy development and implementation are based on reliable, relevant, independent and up-to-date data and research, in order for youth policy to reflect the needs and realities of young people. Explanation: (i) regularly-conducted research on youth; (ii) age-disaggregated data is collected by the MoY, line ministries and independent statistics authority; and (iii) system to facilitate data/information exchange between entity holding the youth portfolio and all other stakeholders involved.
Participatory	Definition: A participatory National Youth Strategy engages all stakeholders, at all stages of the policy cycle, from creation and implementation to monitoring and evaluation. Stakeholders are youth organisations, young people, and all other organisations as well as individuals who are influencing and/or are being influenced by the policy. Particular attention is to be paid to the participation of vulnerable and marginalised groups among all stakeholders. Explanation: (i) meaningful engagement of youth organisations, youth workers and unorganised youth throughout the policy cycle; (ii) variety of tools and channels to ensure meaningful engagement, such as face-to-face meetings, surveys, seminars and conferences, online consultations, and virtual meetings (webinars); and (iii) focused activities to engage vulnerable and marginalized groups.
Resourced / budgeted	Definition: Sufficient resources, both in terms of funding and human resources are available for youth organisations, youth work providers as well as public authorities to develop, implement, monitor and evaluate the National Youth Strategy. Supportive measures, from training schemes to funding programmes, are made available to ensure the capacity building of the actors and structures of youth policy. Explanation: (i) the ministry coordinating the youth portfolio has a dedicated budget; (ii) the ministry coordinating the youth portfolio has sufficient human resources; (iii) a dedicated budget and dedicated staff is assigned to the National Youth Strategy; and (iv) grants and other support structures are made available by the government to youth organisations and youth workers.
Transparent and accessible	Definition: The National Youth Strategy should clearly state which government authority has the overall co-ordinating responsibility for its implementation. It should also be clear which ministries are responsible for the different areas that are addressed in the policy. A transparent policy should be laid out in publicly accessible documents. Explanation: (i) National Youth Strategy available online in an easily accessible website; (ii) the National Youth Strategy clearly defines responsibilities for implementation, monitoring and evaluation; (iii)clear description of roles and responsibilities within the entity coordinating the NYS available and easily accessible to other stakeholders (e.g. organisational chart and contact details); and (iv) results of surveys, consultations and reports are publicly available.
Monitored and evaluated / accountable	Definition: Data is collected in a continual and systematic way. The strategy is systematically and objectively assessed looking at its design, implementation and results with the aim of determining the relevance and fulfilment of objectives, development efficiency, effectiveness, impact and sustainability. An evaluation should provide information that is credible and useful, enabling the incorporation of lessons learned into the decision–making process of both policymakers and intended beneficiaries. Finally, the various stakeholders in the policy making process take responsibility for their actions and can be held accountable for them. Explanation: (i) measurable objectives and targets are set; (ii) key performance indicators linked to the objectives and targets are defined; (iii) a data-collection system for key performance indicators is established; (iv) specific mechanisms exist to ensure the quality of the data collected; (v) progress reports prepared on a regular basis; (vi) evidence produced in monitoring is used to inform decision-making; and (vii) evaluations are prepared regularly and made available.
Cross-sectoral / transversal	Definition: Cross-sectoral youth strategy implies that all relevant policy areas are addressed through youth lenses and there is coordination among different ministries, levels of government and public bodies responsible for and working on issues affecting young people. Explanation: (i) all relevant policy areas are addressed and put in relation with one another in the National Youth Strategy; (ii) line ministries are involved throughout the policy cycle (evidence collection and analysis, drafting, implementation, monitoring and evaluation); (iii) intra-ministerial coordination mechanisms are established; and (iv) mechanisms to involve local and potentially other subnational levels of government throughout the policy cycle of the NYS exist.
Gender responsive	Definition: The National Youth Strategy should be assessed against the specific needs of women and men from diverse backgrounds to ensure inclusive policy outcomes. Explanation: (i) explicit reference to gender equality in the NYS; (ii) availability of gender-disaggregated data; and (iii) availability of gender-specific objectives within the NYS.

Source: OECD.

Brief history of National Youth Strategies in Jordan

In 2004, Jordan was the first country in the MENA region to elaborate a multi-annual National Youth Strategy. Since, at least five more plans were in the phase of development. However, the current National Youth Strategy 2019-25 is the first to be adopted by Cabinet. A review of the draft strategies and the processes that led to their elaboration between 2011 and 2018 illustrates that their implementation failed due to changing political priorities and a number of reoccurring "governance gaps". These shall be discussed briefly below before the section will analyse the NYS 2019-25 against the eight principles of good governance introduced in Table 2.1.

Work on the National Youth Strategy 2005-09 and a corresponding action plan was led by the Higher Council for Youth (predecessor of the Ministry of Youth until 2016, see Chapter 3) in co-operation with international development partners. Drawing on evidence collected through UNICEF's National Youth Survey (2002) and consultations with young people, the strategy targeted youth aged 12-30 years and identified nine thematic priorities. To support its implementation, it recommended the creation of a National Youth Forum for civil society organisations (CSOs) and a Youth Advisory Group. The creation of an inter-ministerial committee and technical committee was expected to facilitate the participation and coordination with line ministries, international partners and organisations affiliated with Jordan's Royal Court. Neither the National Youth Forum for CSOs nor the Youth Advisory Group were created though.

In 2011, the Higher Council for Youth started to work on a second strategy. Efforts were suspended quickly after the available evidence was found to be outdated and the process to lack inclusivity and sustainability, according to the interviews conducted by OECD.[2] A new initiative was started by the Higher Council for Youth a few years later in co-operation with line ministries, non-governmental stakeholders and international partners. The 2014-18 strategy drew on evidence from an evaluation of the 2005-09 strategy and identified nine priority areas. It envisaged the creation of committees to prepare a work plan and steer and oversee its implementation. Due to delays, the strategy later focused on the period 2016-18. Ultimately, however, it was not adopted because relevant stakeholders had not been consulted and its focus was considered to be too general, according to the interviews.

The latest attempt to adopt a multi-year strategy focused on young people resulted in the draft National Youth Empowerment Strategy 2017-25. It laid out five guiding principles and themes and foresaw the elaboration of three-year Action Plans and a monitoring and evaluation system to address the implementation challenges previous strategies exposed. Led by the (new) Ministry of Youth, the strategy was also expected to consolidate its role as "umbrella ministry" for any youth-related initiative and related funding.[3] With the support of international partners, a Steering Committee, stakeholder advisory bodies and an inter-ministerial working group were created to ensure a coordinated approach across various stakeholders. However, as for previous attempts, significant less emphasis was placed on building the necessary capacity and capabilities within the Ministry of Youth to effectively steer and coordinate the process.

Five reoccurring challenges stand out in reviewing previous efforts to adopt and implement a National Youth Strategy in Jordan. First, disruptions due to frequent changes in the political leadership of the Ministry of Youth and changing thematic priorities negatively affected its capacity to plan for the long-term. Second, concerns about outdated or incomplete (age-disaggregated) evidence to inform the identification of priorities and design of programmes frequently delayed or stopped the process. Third, despite the use of different channels to consult young people in the process (e.g. surveys, online questionnaires, meetings in youth centres), there is no evidence about the impact of their contributions. Information gathered during the interviews conducted by OECD also suggest a rather narrow focus on consulting youth that were already registered with the youth centres, raising questions about the inclusiveness of the engagement formats. Fourth, inter-ministerial committees and other bodies set up to work on action plans, oversee implementation and monitor and evaluate progress, ceased to exist.

Finally, somewhat underlying the challenges discussed above, better outcomes were hampered by blurred accountability lines and the fact that no genuine investments were made into skilling up MoY employees and creating sustainable institutional capacities to run and oversee implementation (e.g. systems to gather, transfer and store information; M&E unit). Chapter 3 will discuss the "administrative capacity challenge" but also promising new initiatives taken by the Ministry of Youth to address it, in greater detail.

Findings from the OECD report "Fit for all generations?" highlight that government entities in charge of youth affairs across OECD countries and selected non-members are facing somewhat similar challenges. Across the OECD, only 20% of National Youth Strategies (5 out of 25) are fully participatory, budgeted and monitored and evaluated. Gaps in the governance arrangements can have negative effects for the legitimacy of the strategy, the support and ownership it enjoys by youth stakeholders, and ultimately on programmes and services for young people. Therefore, investments into these arrangements are crucial.

Benchmarking the NYS 2019-25 against eight principles of good governance

The elaboration of the NYS 2019-25 coincided with demonstrations over economic policies, reduced subsidies and the proposed income-tax law in 2018 and 2019. They also merged with renewed demands for a citizen-centred political system and an end to corruption, and new concerns about the enabling environment for youth participation, especially on social media (Chapter 3) (OECD, 2017[14]). In 2018, as per the decision of the Cabinet, the lead on the elaboration of the youth strategy was taken over by a Technical Committee with representatives from the Ministry of Youth, line ministries, non-governmental youth stakeholders and international partners before it was officially launched by Prime Minister Omar Razzaz in July 2019.

The following sections will benchmark Jordan's National Youth Strategy 2019-25 against the eight principles of good governance as presented in OECD's Assessment Framework of National Youth Strategies. It will also provide comparative evidence and good practices from OECD countries in the interest of supporting the achievement of its strategic objectives.

Political commitment: Backed by the Royal Court and Government Plans

High-level political support is critical to generate buy-in across various stakeholders in government and the public and to mobilise resources for the implementation of a youth strategy. Such support can take different shapes, such as statements by the country's leadership, prominent references in government-wide plans or with the location of the youth portfolio within the public administration. In Austria, Colombia and Japan, for instance, units inside the Centre of Government (CoG)[4] steer and coordinate youth affairs across the government. In Germany, the National Youth Strategy was launched jointly by the Head of Government and Minister in charge of youth (OECD, 2020[3]).

Since 2000, the role of the young generation as "the greatest asset and hope for the future" and need for subsequent governments to "tap our young people's intellectual, creative, and reproductive potential in order for Jordan to keep up with new developments in global scientific, economic and social factors" (UNDP, 2000[15]) has been claimed publicly by King Abdullah II. In various Speeches from the Throne and Discussion Papers, he reiterated the importance to involve young people in the development of their country, to listen to their views and to empower youth by developing the state administration and enhancing the rule of law. In this context, King Abdullah II also called for a

> "comprehensive national strategy on youth [...] with the aim of cementing values of good citizenship, the state of law and love of the country. These programmes should also empower young people to realise their potential and expand their horizons and immune them against extremist evil ideologies." (Obeidat, 17 October 2016[16])

The creation of the Crown Prince Foundation in 2015 and its vision to support "Capable youth for an aspiring Jordan" gave new impetus to political reflections upon the situation of youth in Jordan. Around the same time, at global stage, Crown Prince Al Hussein Bin Abdullah II led discussions that resulted in UN

Resolution 2250 – the first to urge countries to increase representation of youth in decision-making at all levels and set up mechanisms to enable young people to participate meaningfully in peace processes and dispute resolution (UN, 2015[17]). In 2016, the transformation of the Higher Council for Youth into the Ministry of Youth marked another important milestone to institutionalise Jordan's ambition to place "youth" high on the political agenda.

The National Youth Strategy 2019-25 places itself in the context of royal directives and strategic government plans, most notably Vision 2025 and government strategies focused on employment (National Employment Strategy 2011-2020; Strategic Plan of the Ministry of Labour 2017-21), economic development (Jordan Economic Catalyzing Growth Plan 2018), poverty reduction (Poverty Reduction Strategy 2013-20), human resource development (National Strategy for Human Resources development 2016-25), social cohesion and sport (Strategy of the Olympic Committee 2018) (Ministry of Youth in Jordan, 2019[1]). It also delivers on Jordan's Renaissance Plan 2019-20 and its commitment to integrate youth in public life and decision making; to develop their democratic culture, citizenship and pluralism; and to review legislation related to increasing the political participation of youth (Government of Jordan, n.d.[18]).

Evidence: Lack of age-disaggregated data and effective information systems

The availability and use of reliable, relevant and up-to-date data is critical to reflect the heterogeneous realities, needs and potential of young people in all relevant policy areas. Jordan's National Youth Strategy 2019-25 acknowledges that programmes and activities in youth centres should be targeted to the specific needs of youth in different governorates. Sound evidence, especially from across the subnational levels of government, is also critical to underpin efforts to monitor and evaluate implementation and to feed the insights from this exercise back into strategic planning and policy making.

To take different circumstances and potential vulnerabilities of youth into account, NYS evidence should be disaggregated by age and identity factors such as gender, socio-economic background, disability and migrant status. Inequalities tend to accumulate over numerous identity factors (e.g. young, female, at risk of poverty) and therefore deserve specific attention by policy makers (OECD, 2017[19]). As a life stage that is characteristic of numerous "transition processes", careful consideration must be given to cover all relevant areas determining youth's wellbeing, including income and wealth, work and job quality, housing, health, knowledge and skills, environmental quality, subjective well-being, safety, work-life-balance, social connections and civil engagement.[5] Averages may mask important disparities between groups and should hence be complemented by evidence on inequalities between groups, between top and bottom performers and with a focus on deprivations (OECD, 2021[20]).

The statistical evidence presented in the NYS 2019-25 is concentrated on a number of high-level indicators on demographics, youth unemployment and the physical infrastructure of youth spaces managed by the Ministry of Youth (e.g. youth centres, youth clubs). Whereas the seven themes and nine strategic objectives of Jordan's NYS cover a wide range of public policy and service areas, the evidence provided to underpin this prioritisation is limited. This is also acknowledged by the SWOT analysis of Jordan's youth sector, which is integrated in the strategy and refers to the lack of specialised studies on youth issues as a "weakness" (Ministry of Youth in Jordan, 2019[1]). Compiling age-disaggregated evidence is also perceived as a challenge by many OECD countries. For instance, among the countries with a National Youth Strategy in place, ministries in charge of youth affairs point to a lack of youth-focused data on the social inclusion of vulnerable groups (45%), youth participation in public life (42%), conflict prevention (36%) and youth rights (36%) (OECD, 2020[3]).

The strategy was informed by a review of royal directives and national strategies, an evaluation of the 2004-09 strategy, international good practices, the SWOT analysis and results of a survey of Jordanian youth, conducted by the General Statistics Department in 2014. Young people were consulted via "tick-the box" opinion polls (targeting age groups 12-18 and 19-30 years) and focus group meetings in 2017. The summary report produced by MoY was not made public. According to the interviews conducted by OECD, evidence was difficult to compile in a number of areas, including youth's participation in volunteering and elections, school drop-outs, health, and the social exclusion of vulnerable groups.

Besides the availability and use of relevant and granular information, the broader IT infrastructure and information systems are critical to facilitate the exchange of data and information across stakeholders (e.g. between the central and subnational level; data storage system, etc.). The lack of an effective data storage system within the Ministry of Youth and at the level of Jordan's 12 governorates (Youth Directorates) is an important impediment to create and transfer institutional memory. Targeted investments into MoY's capacity to collect and use relevant evidence, and in building information systems that facilitate the transfer of information are needed and an important condition to enhance the quality of policy design, implementation, and monitoring and evaluation.

> **Box 2.1. Age-disaggregated evidence in Sweden**
>
> The Swedish Parliament adopted the youth policy bill "With youth in focus: a policy for good living conditions, power and influence" in 2014. The Swedish Agency for Youth and Civil Society (MUCF) is responsible for ensuring that the objectives of the youth policy are achieved. As part of its ongoing effort to monitor and evaluate the youth policy, it continuously compiles and publishes available age-disaggregated data, which is linked to the indicators of the youth policy, on the Ung Idag website (http://www.ungidag.se/) to ensure transparency. It covers six key sectors of interest for youth: work and housing; economic and social vulnerability; physical and mental health; influence and representation; culture and leisure; and training.
>
> Source: (OECD, 2020[3]).

Participatory: Moving from "tick-the-box" to meaningful youth participation

Besides political commitment and evidence, the ambition to deliver youth-responsive policy outcomes requires young people's meaningful participation in the process. Accordingly, the OECD Recommendation on Open Government calls on governments to "grant all stakeholders equal and fair opportunities to be informed and consulted and actively engage them in all phases of the policy-cycle and service design and delivery" (OECD, 2017[8]). Young people's active involvement throughout the different stages increases their ownership and provides a source of heterogeneous ideas and motivations for policy makers to tap upon. It is also critical to ensure the inclusiveness and accountability of policy outcomes. Whereas national youth councils often act as the official representation of young people's interests vis-à-vis government (exist in 77% of OECD countries covered in the 2019 OECD Youth Governance Survey), there is no such body in Jordan (Chapter 4).

Policy makers must take into account the different life circumstances of young people. According to 2018 data from the Pew Research Center, for instance, 93% of 18-29 year old in Jordan own or share a smartphone (85% of the total population). However, this share drops to 76% for the total population with lower than secondary education (Pew Research Center, 2019[21]). Specific attention must be paid to reach out to youth living in remote conditions, poor households and other conditions that put them at high risk of exclusion. A multi-channel approach is needed to involve youth in both virtual and offline formats and target vulnerable groups specifically. This is a significant challenge shared by OECD countries as only 4 out of 10 with a NYS reports that non-organised youth were consulted in the design phase (OECD, 2020[3]).

In turn, findings from the OECD "Fit for all generations?" report indicate that investments into meaningful youth participation in the policy cycle pay off. Figure 2.3 illustrates that youth-led organisations in OECD countries expressed higher satisfaction with the final strategy when they were involved throughout the different stages (e.g. in defining, drafting and reviewing thematic areas) than organisations that were involved ad hoc or not at all.

Figure 2.3. When youth were involved in strategy design, they were more satisfied with results

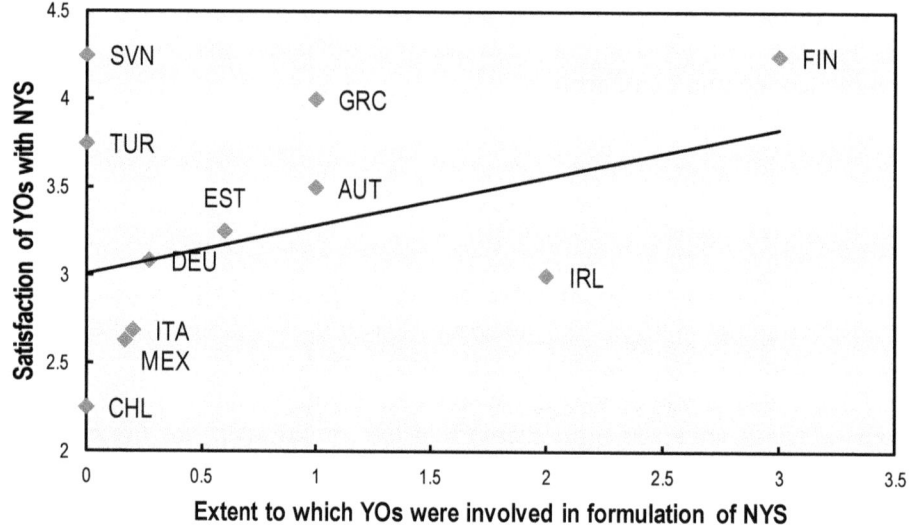

Note: Correlation coefficient: 0.33; p-value: 0.29. The independent variable is the share of youth organisations in each country that indicated to have been consulted to define, draft and review the thematic areas of the National Youth Strategy. The dependent variable is the mean of means of satisfaction expressed by youth organisations with the areas and objectives of the National Youth Strategy.
Source: (OECD, 2020[3]).

The NYS 2019-25 calls for a change in political (and media) attitudes to address the dominance of negative stereotypes in the public discourse about youth. It claims that narratives that identify "youth" as risk or solely beneficiaries of state institutions must be overcome and that, instead, young people's stance in the legislative, political, institutional and social fabric should be encouraged (Ministry of Youth in Jordan, 2019[1]). This shift is a critical condition for meaningful youth participation.

Practically, young people were involved in the elaboration of the strategy via "tick-the-box" opinion polls and focus groups meetings in 2017. Vulnerable youth were not targeted specifically but were, to some extent, represented in the opinion polls and focus groups. The consultations took place in the review phase when the main pillars of the strategy and commitments had been identified. Similarly, while 88% of OECD countries engaged young people in the design of their most recent National Youth Strategy, only every second did so across the full cycle of defining its objectives and priorities, preparing a draft version and reviewing it for final adoption (OECD, 2020[3]). According to the interviews conducted by OECD, young people in Jordan were not informed about whether their input was taken into account. To increase the transparency and accountability of the participatory process, Canada and New Zealand published specific summary reports of young people's inputs, which were made public (OECD, 2020[3]).

As further discussed in Chapter 4, the opportunities for young people to shape programming in the youth centres at local level is also rather limited.

> **Box 2.2. Participatory approaches to youth policy in selected OECD countries**
>
> **The Child and Youth Wellbeing Strategy in New Zealand**
>
> The Child and Youth Wellbeing Strategy in New Zealand benefited from the contributions of 10,000 New Zealanders, including 6,000 children and young people. The Government used a wide range of mechanisms, including face-to-face interviews, focus groups, workshops, academic forums and surveys.
>
> The inclusion of children and young people from vulnerable groups, especially young Māori and other pacific young people as well as disabled youth, young women, refugees or children in care of the state, was a priority. The government also consulted a reference group, made up of child and youth representatives, including non-governmental organisations and academics, and published reports online to report back on the feedback received.
>
> **Special Youth Rapporteurs in Japan**
>
> The Japanese Cabinet Office appoints students as "Special Youth Rapporteurs" to inform government planning, legislation and regulations related to childhood and youth. The Special Youth Rapporteurs are asked to give their opinion on government thematic priorities, which are selected by the Cabinet Office. Their inputs are then shared across relevant ministries and government agencies and are published online on the website of the Cabinet Office.
>
> Source: (OECD, 2020[3]).

Resourced / budgeted: Matching political commitment with investments in MoY

Adequate financial, human and technical resources must be provided to ensure the successful implementation of the National Youth Strategy. This concerns the internal capacity of the government entity in charge of steering the strategy and the support provided to implementation partners, for instance youth/community-based organisations, youth workers and non-governmental service providers. Such support can take the form of financial support (e.g. through grants for youth-led initiatives), training and capacity building and physical infrastructure (e.g. youth centres), among others. While the MoY does not provide direct financial support to the third sector in Jordan, it supports youth clubs and affiliated associations. Findings from the OECD report "Fit for all generations?" suggests that adequate financial resources can facilitate coordination across government entities, however, only 17 of 25 NYS are backed by earmarked funding (OECD, 2020[3]).

According to the Ministry of Youth, as of May 2021, Jordanian Dinar (JOD) 500,000 (around USD 705,000) have been allocated by its budget to the implementation of the strategy. Reportedly, in the context of the COVID-19 pandemic and closed youth centres, activities in 2019 and 2020 were implemented primarily virtually.[6] Partnerships with national and international partners was expected to secure additional funding and implementation support. As will be discussed further in Chapter 3, the limited budget for youth programming is one of the key challenges faced by MoY, as is also recognised by the SWOT analysis that informed the elaboration of the strategy (Ministry of Youth in Jordan, 2019[1]).

The Ministry of Youth is the main or co-responsible entity for around two-thirds of all projects covered by the strategy. The ministries of education, labour, information and communication technology are each involved in four projects, the ministries of health and Awqaf Islamic Affairs and Holy Places in three, and the ministries of culture, environment and public works and housing in one, respectively. Implementing partners are expected to include projects in their respective strategic plans, identify necessary resources, prepare operational plans and monitor financial costs (Ministry of Youth in Jordan, 2019[1]). However, as of May 2021, it is unclear if line ministries have mobilised financial resources to deliver on the NYS's objectives.

In terms of human resource capacity to deliver on the strategy, both employees at the central level and subnational level (e.g. Youth Directors, managers of youth centres) play a crucial role. Chapter 3 finds that only 36 out of 1881 employees at the ministry work in the General or Local Administration whereas most staff fulfils support functions. Moreover, employees working in the youth centres, who are expected to play an important role in rolling out programmes and initiatives, do not always have the qualifications to work with young people according to the interviews conducted by OECD. This is also acknowledged by the NYS 2019-25, which lists "poor efficiency of human resources working with young people" as a challenge (Ministry of Youth in Jordan, 2019[1]).

Trainings provided by the Youth Leadership Centre, the internal capacity building arm at MoY, do not include activities to skill up employees in the design, implementation and monitoring and evaluation of policy or programmes. Limited financial and human resource capacity to steer the NYS 2019-25 presents a risk and points to a more fundamental need to invest in building administrative capacity within MoY in order to mitigate dependency on external support (see Chapter 3).

Transparent and accessible

Easy access to the strategy is crucial to promote transparency and public scrutiny, and ultimately youth's trust in government. In turn, the strategy can serve as a communication tool for government to demonstrate how it translates high-level political commitments into youth-responsive programmes and services.

The NYS 2019-25 is available on the website of the ministry in Arabic and English and can be downloaded (Ministry of Youth in Jordan, 2019[22]). No public information is available in terms of the distribution of roles and responsibilities within MoY. For instance, the Organisation Chart available on the website[7] does not specify which thematic division(s) will be in charge, nor does a "who is who" section with contact information exists. There is also no information about the progress achieved in implementing the strategy, for instance in the form of an annual report or list of ongoing and completed initiatives to deliver on its objectives. Across OECD countries with a National Youth Strategy in place, 88% publish the results of monitoring and evaluation exercises. The most common channel used is the ministry website (60%), followed by annual reports available to the public (32%). 6% of government entities in charge of steering the youth strategy use the entity's social media account for this purpose (OECD, 2020[3]).

In line with Jordan's strategic efforts to foster open, transparent and accountable policy making through the Open Government Partnership (OGP), MoY could generate quick wins by publishing a description of the respective teams, tasks and contact information along with the results of the youth consultation exercise, among others.

Monitored and evaluated / accountable

The Ministry of Youth is designated to monitor and evaluate the implementation of the strategic objectives and projects of the NYS 2019-25, based on the periodic submission of progress reports by its implementing partners. The consolidated progress report shall be submitted by MoY to the Prime Minister for information and guidance (Ministry of Youth in Jordan, 2019[1]). This is aligned with the practices in most OECD countries where the government entity in charge of coordinating the youth portfolio also leads on monitoring (82%) and evaluation (65%) (OECD, 2020[3]).

Each project in the NYS 2019-25 is linked to a strategic, sectorial and national objective and theme, Key Performance Indicators (KPIs), mostly at the level of outputs (e.g. number of trainings), and implementation period. While links to outcome indicators and impact are less pronounced, the focus on measuring performance shows important progress compared to earlier drafts. The decentralised approach to monitor and evaluate performance can create a sense of shared ownership and accountability among implementation partners if quality standards are met and adequate M&E capacities exist in the respective entities.

Figure 2.4 illustrates the mechanisms put in place by OECD countries and selected non-member countries to monitor and evaluate National Youth Strategies. Around two-thirds of National Youth Strategies in OECD countries set measurable objectives and targets, prepare periodic progress reports (i.e. at least annually) and reports to feed information from the M&E exercise back into the policy making cycle. One in two identifies KPIs linked to objectives and targets and is embedded in a data collection system to track progress. On the other hand, one in four youth strategies is monitored and evaluated on an ad hoc basis and only 8% of OECD countries have put in place specific mechanisms to ensure the quality of evidence (e.g. quality control mechanism).

Figure 2.4. Monitoring and evaluation of National Youth Strategies, OECD and selected countries

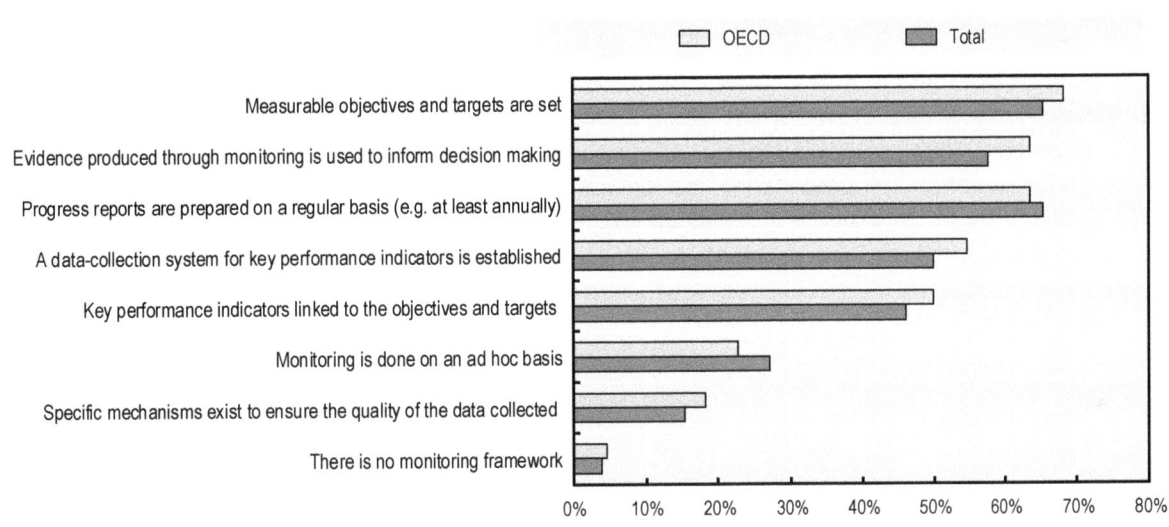

Note: Total refers to 26 countries, which consist of 22 OECD member and 4 non-member countries that have a NYS. OECD refers to 22 countries.
Source: (OECD, 2020[3]).

As of May 2021, the Institutional Performance and Development Unit in the MoY is in charge of monitoring and evaluating the strategy in Jordan. According to the Ministry of Youth, a team of managers was formed to lead the process and to submit regular reports to the Prime Minister's Office. In line with OECD recommendations presented in a high-level roundtable meeting on 5 March 2020 in Amman[8], an evaluation study was conducted and trainings were organised with the support of USAID to strengthen its monitoring and evaluation capacity.[9] Investments in this area present an important step to increase accountability and could be accompanied by trainings in strategic planning and evidence-based policy making for designated employees in the future.

According to MoY, a detailed report was prepared on the implementation of programmes and activities by the Ministry of Youth for 2020, including quantitative indicators focused on the number of programmes delivered by Directorates and on the participation of male and female youth in the activities. The report lists ten findings and recommendations, most notably to link the activities in the Youth Directorates and youth centres to the strategic pillars of the NYS 2019-25 and to strengthen reporting practices, most notably through quarterly reports. It also underlines the importance to ensure gender parity in the access to the activities and balanced distribution across all governorates.[10] However, also due to the exceptional circumstances of the COVID-19 pandemic, none of the implementing partners have submitted their reports to the Ministry of Youth as of May 2021[11]. Despite the significant impact of the crisis, there is no information available if an update of the strategy and its activities and targets is planned.

The Ministry of Youth reports that a meeting with implementing partners was held in 2021 through the Steering Committee (headed by the Minister of Youth, gathering Secretary-Generals from line ministries and other implementing partners[12]) to reinforce mechanisms of follow-up, evaluation and impact measurements of the programmes and activities of the NYS 2019-25. Available information by the Ministry of Youth suggests that the Technical Committee, headed by MoY's Secretary-General and gathering liaison officers from line ministries and other implementing partners, is still in the process of being created. Implementing partners were requested to prepare implementation plans covering a detailed description of programmes, activities, performance indicators and other stakeholders involved in their implementation.[13] Upholding regular meetings of the Steering Committee/Technical Committee will play an important role in building cross-ministerial support and accountability for the implementation of the NYS 2019-25. Besides, the Ministry of Youth could consider undertaking a mid-term evaluation report to track progress and identify opportunities of addressing existing shortcomings (e.g. lack of implementation plans among its partners) and reinforcing ongoing efforts to strengthen internal capacities in this area (e.g. data collection system, skills and knowledge of its employees).

To further strengthen the M&E system in the youth sector in Jordan, these efforts could be complemented by a more prominent role being played by independent institutions (e.g. independent commissions, Supreme Audit Institutions, Ombudsperson), the legislature and young people (OECD, 2020[23]). Notably, the OECD report "Fit for all generations?" finds that youth's active involvement in monitoring and evaluating the youth strategy can increase their satisfaction with public policy and service delivery. Box 2.3 illustrates different approaches adopted by OECD countries to involve independent institutions, parliament and young people in these efforts.

Box 2.3. Mechanisms to monitor and evaluate youth policy and programmes in OECD countries

In **Finland**, the National Audit Office examined the results and effectiveness of youth workshops in 2013–2016, and the allocation of the resources and cost efficiency of youth work in 2014–2017 (National Audit Office of Finland, 2020[24]).

In **Costa Rica**, the results of the evaluation exercise are presented to the National Youth Assembly, which is tasked with approving the National Youth Strategy. The Assembly is composed of representatives of different civil society organisations, universities, political parties and ethnic groups and meets on a regular basis.

In the **Slovak Republic**, the Strategy for Youth (2014-20) was monitored and evaluated by two expert groups: an inter-ministerial working group for state policy in the field of youth, co-ordinated by the Ministry of Education, Science, Research and Sport, and the Committee for Children and Youth, co-ordinated by the Ministry of Labour, Social Affairs and Family. Progress reports are elaborated yearly and submitted to the relevant Minister. In parallel, young people and non-governmental organisations were involved through public consultations at national and regional level. This led to the elaboration of a mid-term evaluation "Youth Report" in 2018 and a final report to evaluate the progress and impact of the strategy is expected to be submitted in 2021.

Source: (OECD, 2020[3]).

Cross-sectoral / transversal

The cross-cutting nature of youth policy requires effective coordination mechanisms and mandates to ensure a coherent approach in the delivery of policies, programmes and services to youth. To create a sense of shared ownership and accountability, mandates and limits thereof need to be transparent, comprehensive and clearly identified for each. The NYS 2019-25 underlines the need to strengthen cross-sectoral coordination in the youth sector in Jordan. It identifies as challenges the duplication of efforts, a narrow focus on specific segments of youth and the lack of a holistic mapping of the situation of youth, programmes, institutions, mandates, funds and performance information (Ministry of Youth in Jordan, 2019[1]).

The NYS 2019-25 focuses on seven policy areas. It covers many of the areas that are prominently addressed by National Youth Strategies across OECD countries, too (see Figure Figure 2.5). Notably, all OECD countries with a NYS in place cover "youth participation in public life", 96% feature commitments on "employment/economy" and "education/training", 92% do so for "health" and 84% for the social inclusion of vulnerable groups, and sports/culture/leisure. In contrast, while the social inclusion of vulnerable groups (84%), youth rights (76%), transportation (52%) and mental health are also addressed prominently by most youth strategies across the OECD countries, they are not covered explicitly by the NYS 2019-25.

Figure 2.5. Thematic focus of National Youth Strategies, OECD and selected countries

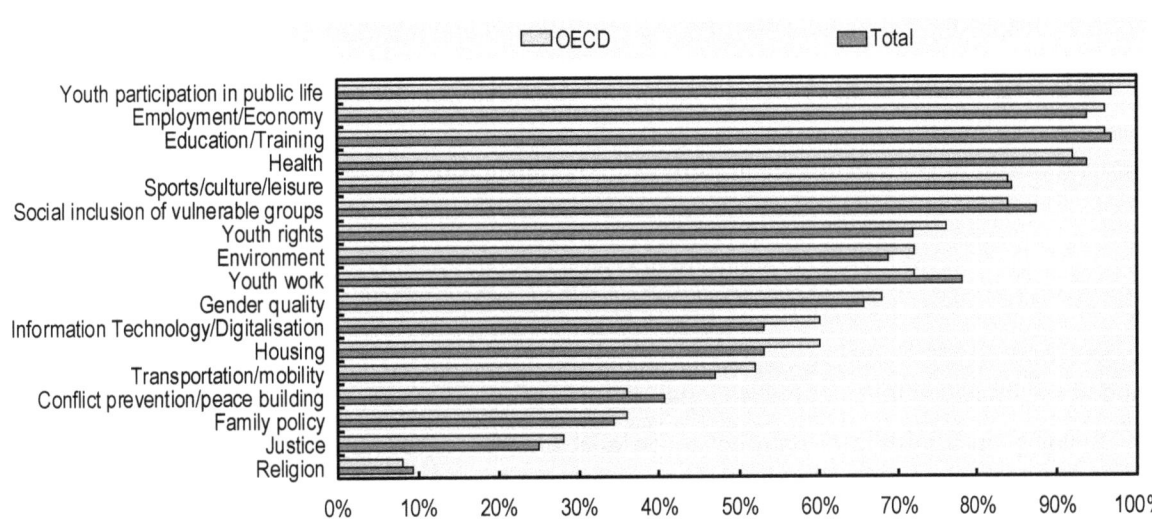

Note: Total refers to 32 countries, which consist of 25 OECD member and 7 non-member countries that have or are elaborating a NYS. OECD refers to 25 countries.
Source: (OECD, 2020[3]).

Among a total of 99 implementing partners, the NYS 2019-25 distinguishes between governmental (49), non-governmental (24) and international (26) stakeholders, covering (entities affiliated to) the Royal Court (e.g. Crown Prince Foundation), national parliament, Jordan's justice and security apparatus, independent institutions, private sector, non-for-profit associations and entities focused on the civil service workforce, human rights, and training and employment. To ensure alignment across sectors, royal directives and government programmes in the area of education, scientific research, employment, poverty reduction and human resource development were reviewed (Ministry of Youth in Jordan, 2019[1]).

The diversity of thematic areas covered and implementing partners from various backgrounds identified can be a core strength of the NYS 2019-25. At the same time, a genuine cross-sectoral approach relies on strong institutional mechanisms to bring different partners together on a regular basis and ensure coherence in youth programming. Available information provided by the Ministry of Youth suggests that the Steering Committee has met once in 2021 whereas the Technical Committee has not been set up yet. The full operationalisation of these two bodies could be considered a priority by the Ministry of Youth in order to elaborate implementation plans, identify funding requirements and track progress achieved by the respective implementing partners.

Gender responsive

Young people in Jordan constitute a highly heterogeneous group of people that are not only defined by their age but also other identity factors, such as gender, socio-economic background, disability and migrant status, and many more. Taking into account intersecting identity factors in policy and programme design, implementation and monitoring and evaluation is important to anticipate increased risks of vulnerability and marginalisation among the youth cohort.

The NYS 2019-25 acknowledges that youth should not be viewed as a single block. Instead, it calls for targeted programmes for each governorate and judiciary to meet the diverse priorities and concerns of young people (Ministry of Youth in Jordan, 2019[1]). It covers five projects that are targeted at young people with a disability, for instance to improve their integration into the educational process (Project 1.7) and activities in the youth centres (Project 5.3). Missing, on the other hand, are dedicated projects focused on youth from difficult socio-economic backgrounds and young people living in poverty. Migrant and refugee youth are also not explicitly covered by the strategies' projects.

Furthermore, despite their increased risk of being unemployed and face barriers to participate in public life, the NYS 2019-25 does not cover specific objectives for young women. In turn, while girls outperform boys in school in Jordan, the NYS 2019-25 and its targets generally refer to all young people. A potential mid-term evaluation of the strategy could place a particular focus on its impact for vulnerable and marginalised youth groups to inform more targeted programming for these groups in the future.

Recommendations

To support the implementation of the National Youth Strategy 2019-25, consider to:

- Building up a system of data collection and storage, including at the subnational level, and setting clear quality standards for submitting evidence from governmental and non-governmental partners to monitor and evaluate the implementation of MoY's strategic objectives.
- Collecting age-disaggregated data systematically across all relevant policy areas in combination with other identity factors in partnership with the Department of Statistics, universities or the private sector.
- Creating a mechanism for young people and youth-led organisations to support the implementation of the strategy as well as Jordan's response and recovery plans to mitigate the COVID-19 crisis, creating adequate organisational and technical support.
- Creating a monitoring and evaluation unit and building capacities among MoY employees to identify key performance indicators, monitor implementation and evaluate outputs, outcomes and impact of the strategy.

- Fully operationalising the Steering Committee and creating a technical committee in order to develop implementation plans, identify funding requirements and clarify monitoring and evaluation duties for all governmental and non-governmental partners.

References

Government of Jordan (n.d.), *Jordan Renaissance Plan*, https://your.gov.jo/ (accessed on 24 May 2021). [18]

Milton-Edwards, B. (2018), *Marginalized youth: Toward an inclusive Jordan*, https://www.brookings.edu/wp-content/uploads/2018/06/June-2018_Beverly-Jordan_English-Web.pdf (accessed on 24 May 2021). [6]

Ministry of Youth in Jordan (2019), *National Youth Strategy 2019-2025*, http://moy.gov.jo/sites/default/files/jordan_national_youth_strategy_2019-2025_english_compressed_1.pdf (accessed on 12 May 2021). [1]

Ministry of Youth in Jordan (2019), *National Youth Strategy 2019-25*, http://moy.gov.jo/?q=ar/node/2769 (accessed on 15 May 2021). [22]

National Audit Office of Finland (2020), *Effectiveness of youth workshops, and resources and efficiency of outreach youth work*, https://www.vtv.fi/en/publications/effectiveness-of-youth-workshops-and-resources-and-efficiency-of-outreach-youth-work/ (accessed on 15 May 2021). [24]

Obeidat, O. (17 October 2016), *Analysts say solution to wasta is easy: enforce the law*, http://jordantimes.com/news/local/analysts-say-solution-wasta-easy-enforce-law (accessed on 24 May 2021). [16]

OECD (2021), *Measuring Well-being and Progress: Well-being Research*, https://www.oecd.org/statistics/measuring-well-being-and-progress.htm (accessed on 13 May 2021). [20]

OECD (2020), *Governance for Youth, Trust and Intergenerational Justice: Fit for All Generations?*, OECD Public Governance Reviews, OECD Publishing, Paris, https://dx.doi.org/10.1787/c3e5cb8a-en. [3]

OECD (2020), *Improving Governance with Policy Evaluation: Lessons From Country Experiences*, OECD Publishing, https://dx.doi.org/10.1787/89b1577d-en (accessed on 15 May 2021). [23]

OECD (2020), *Schooling disrupted, schooling rethought: How the Covid-19 pandemic is changing education*, https://www.oecd-ilibrary.org/education/schooling-disrupted-schooling-rethought-how-the-covid-19-pandemic-is-changing-education_68b11faf-en (accessed on 7 June 2021). [2]

OECD (2020), *Youth and COVID-19: Response, Recovery and Resilience*, https://read.oecd-ilibrary.org/view/?ref=134_134356-ud5kox3g26&title=Youth-and-COVID-19-Response-Recovery-and-Resilience (accessed on 22 July 2020). [5]

OECD (2019), *OECD Draft Policy Framework on Sound Public Governance*, https://www.oecd.org/gov/draft-policy-framework-on-sound-public-governance.pdf (accessed on 12 May 2021). [13]

OECD (2019), *Recommendation of the Council on Policy Coherence for Sustainable Development*, https://www.oecd.org/gov/pcsd/recommendation-on-policy-coherence-for-sustainable-development-eng.pdf (accessed on 29 March 2020). [12]

OECD (2018), *Youth Engagement and Empowerment*, https://www.oecd.org/mena/governance/youth-engagement-and-empowerment-report.pdf (accessed on 12 May 2021). [4]

OECD (2017), *Engaging Citizens in Jordan's Local Government Needs Assessment Process*, https://www.oecd-ilibrary.org/governance/engaging-citizens-in-jordan-s-local-government-needs-assessment-process_c3bddbcb-en (accessed on 8 June 2021). [14]

OECD (2017), *Recommendation of the Council on Open Government*, https://www.oecd.org/gov/Recommendation-Open-Government-Approved-Council-141217.pdf (accessed on 22 July 2020). [8]

OECD (2017), *Update Report 2017 - Inclusive Growth*, https://www.oecd.org/mcm/documents/C-MIN-2017-3-EN.pdf (accessed on 14 May 2021). [19]

OECD (2016), *2015 OECD Recommendation of the Council on Gender Equality in Public Life*, OECD Publishing, Paris, https://dx.doi.org/10.1787/9789264252820-en. [9]

OECD (2016), *Youth in the MENA Region: How to Bring Them In*, OECD Publishing, Paris, https://dx.doi.org/10.1787/9789264265721-en. [7]

OECD (2015), *Recommendation of the Council on Budgetary Governance*, https://www.oecd.org/gov/budgeting/Recommendation-of-the-Council-on-Budgetary-Governance.pdf (accessed on 12 May 2021). [11]

OECD (2014), *Centre Stage: Driving Better Policies from the Centre of Government*, https://www.oecd.org/gov/Centre-Stage-Report.pdf (accessed on 13 May 2021). [25]

OECD (2012), *Recommendation of the Council on Regulatory Policy and Governance*, https://www.oecd.org/gov/regulatory-policy/49990817.pdf (accessed on 26 April 2020). [10]

Pew Research Center (2019), *Mobile Connectivity in Emerging Economies*, https://www.pewresearch.org/internet/wp-content/uploads/sites/9/2019/03/PI_2019.03.07_Mobile-Connectivity_FINAL.pdf (accessed on 14 May 2021). [21]

UN (2015), *Resolution 2250*, https://undocs.org/en/S/RES/2250(2015) (accessed on 13 May 2021). [17]

UNDP (2000), *Jordan Human Development Report 2000: The Youth of Jordan*, http://hdr.undp.org/sites/default/files/nhdr_2000_jordan-en.pdf (accessed on 13 May 2021). [15]

Notes

[1] As of May 2021, according to available information, only Jordan, Kuwait, the Palestinian Authority and United Arab Emirates (National Youth Agenda) have an operational National Youth Strategy or similar government plan in place. The youth strategy in Morocco is not yet adopted by Cabinet. At least six MENA countries (Algeria, Bahrain, Egypt, Mauritania, Oman, Tunisia) are in the process of elaborating a youth strategy, whereas five countries do not have one (Iraq, Libya, Saudi Arabia, Syria, Yemen). Qatar's National Development Strategy (2018-2022) on "Cultural Enrichment and Sports Excellence" features a pillar on youth empowerment and sports excellence. The status of the Youth Policy in Lebanon, which was endorsed in 2012, is unclear.

[2] Interviews conducted with employees of the Ministry of Youth in Jordan in 2019.

[3] Presentation delivered by representatives from the Ministry of Youth on 5 September 2016 in Paris.

[4] The Centre of Government (through the offices of Prime Ministers and Presidents) can generate political will and leadership to pursue a cross-sectorial approach across different ministries and different levels of government (OECD, 2014[25]). Findings from the 2019 OECD Youth Governance Surveys demonstrate the "coordination" was not perceived as a challenge by any of the countries in which youth affairs are chiefly being dealt with by the CoG.

[5] The policy areas represent the dimensions of the OECD wellbeing framework (current wellbeing) (OECD, 2021[20]).

[6] Information provided by the Ministry of Youth on 24 May 2021.

[7] http://moy.gov.jo/?q=ar/node/23

[8] The roundtable meeting was organised with the member of the Steering Committee of the project "Youth in Public Life in Jordan" to discuss the key findings from the OECD assessment. It gathered the Minister of Youth, representatives from seven lines ministries and 10 non-governmental stakeholders/international partners alongside the Ambassadors of Italy, Switzerland and UK to Jordan and Embassy representatives from Canada, European Commission, France, Japan, Netherlands, Spain and United States.

[9] Information provided by the Ministry of Youth on 24 May 2021.

[10] The report lists among its recommendation to link the activities of Youth Directorates at subnational level to the strategic pillars and objectives of the NYS 2019-25; to ensure an equal participation of young men and women in MoY's activities; and to promote the distribution of activities across all governorates. It also calls for Youth Directorates to provide the ministry with quarterly reports on the implementation of activities based on output indicators such as the total number of beneficiaries and share of men/women. Similarly, it notes that Action Plans should be prepared with the implementing partners, who, in turn, should inform the Ministry about their activities to support the implementation of the NYS 2019-25. It also calls for regular meetings of the Steering Committee to discuss challenges and accomplishments.

[11] Idem.

[12] The Steering Committee is composed of the Secretary Generals of the Ministry of Youth, Ministry of Culture, Ministry of Education, Ministry of Higher Education and Scientific Research, Ministry of Political

and Parliamentary Affairs, Ministry of Digital Economy and Entrepreneurship, Ministry of Endowments and Islamic Affairs, Ministry of Labour, as well as representatives from the Prime Minister's Office, the Ministry of Media Affairs, the Ministry of the Interior, and the General Command of the Armed Forces.

3 Building administrative capacity to deliver for youth in Jordan

This chapter examines the formal organisation of youth affairs in Jordan with a focus on the administrative capacities within the Ministry of Youth. It will analyse the coordination mechanisms established horizontally (across ministerial departments) and vertically (across the different levels of government) to translate the ministry's strategic objectives into programmes and activities across the governorates. Based on an overview of innovation in governance to mainstream youth concerns in policy making across MENA and OECD countries, it will point to good practices and lessons learned that could be applied in Jordan.

Administrative capacities matter to deliver policies, programmes and services that are responsive to the diverse needs of young people. However, as a recent OECD report across more than 40 countries demonstrates, the financial and human resources at the government entity steering youth policy and programming are often weak (OECD, 2020[1]).

In Jordan, the transformation of the Higher Council for Youth into the Ministry of Youth in 2016 was perceived as a signal to place the concerns of young people higher on the political agenda[1]. With the adoption of the National Youth Strategy 2019-25 in 2019, Jordan has made an important step in consolidating the role of the ministry, however, capacity challenges continue to persist (Chapter 2).

This Chapter discusses the formal organisation of youth affairs in Jordan with a focus on the administrative capacity that is available within the Ministry of Youth. Based on the initial assessment of existing coordination mechanisms to implement the NYS 2019-25 in Chapter 2, it will analyse to what extent the ministry's strategic objectives are coordinated horizontally (across ministerial departments) and vertically (across the different levels of government). The Chapter will build on the self-assessment of strengths, weaknesses, opportunities and threats (SWOT), conducted by the Ministry of Youth in the context of elaborating the National Youth Strategy 2019-25, and provide further insights based on the interviews conducted by the OECD and documents made available by MoY's Institutional Development Unit. It will complement the analysis with good practice examples from across MENA and OECD countries.

Organisation of youth affairs at the central level

As stipulated by Regulation No. (78) of 2016[2], the Ministry of Youth is mandated to entertain communication channels between the government and youth, develop youth's skills and abilities, and to coordinate between all entities supporting youth. The ministry is also in charge of designing and implementing youth policies and programmes to ensure their integration and participation in political, social and cultural life and of maintaining and rehabilitating sports facilities. Under its auspices, the law foresees that youth initiatives and entities shall be organised, and that the its youth centres shall be revitalised (Prime Ministry Official Website, 2021[2]).

Table 3.1 demonstrates that, across selected MENA governments, "youth affairs" are most commonly led by a dedicated ministry of combined portfolios, notably "youth" and "sports". Whereas, historically, the focus on "sport" has been more dominant in many countries, recent years have seen renewed efforts to elaborate National Youth Strategies and invest in youth prgramming (Chapter 2). Other than the name suggests, the Ministry of Youth in Jordan covers both youth affairs and sports.

Table 3.1. Bodies with formal responsibility for youth affairs in selected MENA governments, 2021

Country	Ministry	Entity within the Ministry
Algeria	Ministry of Youth and Sports	The General Directorate for Youth Affairs
Bahrain	Ministry of Youth and Sports Affairs	Youth Empowerment Directorate
Egypt	Ministry of Youth and Sports	Youth Directorate
Iraq	Ministry of Youth and Sports	Youth, culture and Art Department
Jordan	Ministry of Youth	The General Directorate for Youth Affairs
Lebanon	Ministry of Youth and Sports	Youth Department
Mauritania	Ministry of Employment, Youth and Sports	General Directorate for Youth

Country	Ministry	Entity within the Ministry
Morocco	**Ministry of Youth and Sports**	Directorate of Youth and Children and Women Affairs
Palestinian Authority	**Higher Council for Youth and Sports**	The General Directorate for Youth Affairs
Tunisia	**Ministry of Youth, Sports and Professional Integration**	The General Directorate for Youth

Note: The principal entity responsible for youth policy and programme co-ordination in each country is shown in **bold**.
Source: (Youth Policy, 2021[3]), (Youth Policy, 2021[4]), (Ministry of Youth and Sports Affairs, 2021[5]) (Ministry of Youth and Sports, 2021[6]), (Ministry of Youth and Sports, 2021[7]), (Ministry of Youth and Sports, 2021[8]), (Higher Council for Youth and Sports, 2021[9]), (Ministry of Youth, 2021[10]), (Ministry of Youth and Sports, 2021[11]) , (Ministry of Youth and Sports, 2021[12]), (Ministry of Employment, 2021[13])

In turn, OECD countries have adopted four different approaches to manage and coordinate youth-focused policies, programmes and services: (1) at the Centre of Government (CoG)[3] (i.e. Austria, Colombia and Japan); (2) in a dedicated ministry, often covering other portfolios such as education, sports and family affairs (e.g. Czech Republic, Italy and Germany); (3) in a department or office within a ministry in charge of combined portfolios (e.g. Sweden, Finland, France); or (4) through a mainstreamed approach, in the absence of a single national authority responsible for youth affairs such as in Denmark.

The most common form of organising youth affairs across OECD countries (19) is through a dedicated unit or department inside a ministry, primarily the ministry in charge of education (OECD, 2020[1]) (OECD, 2018[14]). The OECD report "Governance for Youth, Trust and Intergenerational Justice: Fit for all generations?" finds that countries in which the youth portfolio is located at the CoG find it less challenging to secure political commitment to co-ordinate and implement youth policy, programmes and services (OECD, 2020[1]).

Figure 3.1 displays the Organisational Chart of the Ministry of Youth in Jordan. Administratively, the youth and sports portfolios within the ministry are managed by two distinct directorates. Whereas the Directorate of Youth Clubs and Associations is in charge of "sports", the Directorate for Youth Affairs is responsible for "youth". Besides sports and youth programming, the Ministry of Youth manages five youth and sports cities and oversees the work of the Youth Directorates across Jordan's governorates as well as in Petra. The work of the Directorate for Youth Affairs, the Institutional Performance Development Unit, all youth cities except for the Al Hussein Youth City, and the Youth Directorates in the governorates is formally overseen by the Secretary General.

Figure 3.1. Organisational Chart of the Ministry of Youth, Jordan, 2021

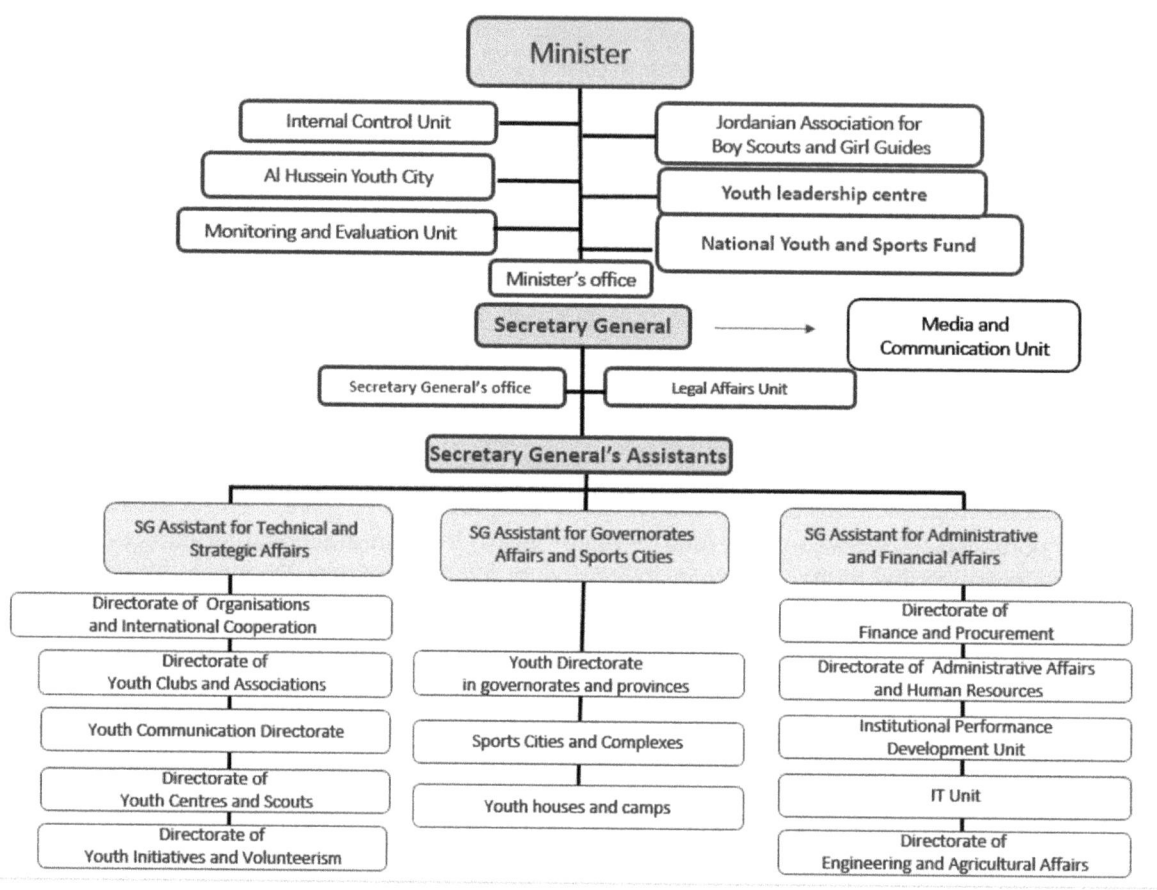

Note: The figure shows the legal entities of the Ministry of Youth, as stipulated in Article 3 of the regulation No. (78) Of 2016.
Source: OECD analysis based on available data provided by the Ministry of Youth in Jordan

The International Cooperation Department is the main interlocutor for projects that are implemented with the support of international partners. The Institutional Performance Development Unit is in charge of strategic planning, administrative and organisational development, services and operations development, as well as for monitoring and evaluating the National Youth Strategy[4]. It therefore plays an important role to ensure adequate administrative capacities and effective governance structures for the ministry to deliver on its mandate. In 2021, the Ministry elaborated the Strategic and Institutional Development Strategy (2021-24). Among the main objectives of the strategy, it identifies building institutional capacities inside the Ministry of Youth; increasing the skills and competencies of its staff; updating and developing legislation and manuals to provide more flexibility and decentralised procedures and simplifying procedures[5].

In terms of strategic planning, the Minister is assisted and advised by the Committee for Planning, Coordination and Follow-up, which the Minister presides. It gathers the Secretary-General and the Directors of the National Youth and Sports Fund; Hussein Youth City, the Youth Leadership Centre and up to two directors (Official Gazette, 2016[15])[6]. The committee is in charge of studying and submitting recommendations to the Minister on the plans, programmes and activities of the ministry, including for drafting laws and regulations and spending decisions, including the preparation of the annual budget and the definition of job descriptions.

Other important entities within the ministry include the National Youth and Sports Fund and the Youth Leadership Centre. The Youth Leadership Centre is in charge of organising and implementing trainings and workshops for its employees to build capacity and enhance leadership skills. The Minister also supervises the Jordanian Association for Boy Scouts and Girl Guides, which was established in 1987 to educate the local community in the field of health awareness and education. The work of the Ministry is supported by departments in charge of administrative affairs, financial affairs, engineering and agricultural affairs, media, legal affairs and IT. As reported by the Ministry in 2020, it oversees the infrastructure and work of 190 youth centres (106 for young men and 84 for young women), 21 youth houses and hostels, 22 youth complexes, 7 youth camps, and 355 youth clubs.

The main role of Jordan's youth centres is to empower young people, promote resilient societies and assess the challenges and opportunities young people face. As defined by the NYS 2019-25, youth centers are "''youth spaces" to activate their role in "attracting the local community, creating ways of real communication with young workers, building relationships with them to develop youth work and achieve the goal of empowering Jordanian youth (Chapter 4)." Another key role of youth centres is to encourage and institutionalise active, successful and influential youth initiatives (Ministry of Youth, 2019[16]).

Building skills for youth-responsive policy making and programming

The development of the capacities of civil servants is essential to design better policies and regulations, to work effectively with citizens and service users, to commission cost-effective service delivery, and to collaborate with stakeholders in networked settings (OECD, 2017[17]). Ensuring that civil servants working for and with youth have the right skills and capabilities for an increasingly digital and globalised world is thus crucial to deliver inclusive policy outcomes and keep pace with national and international developments.

The National Youth Strategy 2019-25 points out that further investments in the skills and capacities of MoY's employees are needed, in particular among employees who are working directly with young people, notably staff in the youth centres (Ministry of Youth, 2019[16]). The interviews conducted by OECD with MoY officials and young people in the youth centres reaffirm the need for targeted training opportunities.

Few MoY employees work on youth policy and programming

In 2020, the Ministry of Youth employed 1881 staff, including employees operating across its youth centres and youth and sports cities. The workforce is categorised along six job categories. Accordingly, the vast majority (52%) holds "Supportive Jobs", followed by "Other jobs" (37%), which are not further defined, and "Accountants" (7%). In turn, only 36 employees (2%) are considered part of the "General Administration and Local Administration", which covers senior managers and other senior positions with responsibility to design and run youth-focused policies, programmes and services (See Figure 1.2). The low share of employees with a background in policy making and youth programming is one of the main challenges faced by the ministry (Ministry of Youth, 2019[16]). In addition, the SWOT Analysis conducted by the Ministry of Youth as part of the Strategic and Institutional Development Strategy (2021-24) acknowledges the lack of qualified human resources as a weakness[7].

As of 2020, only 35% of employees in the Ministry of Youth are women, down from 42% in 2018. This compares to a share of 50% of female government workforce (all civil servants) in Jordan (OECD, 2017[17]). The most significant gender gap exists in the job category "General Administrators and/or Local Administrators" as only 2 out of 36 employees are women (General Budget Department, 2020[18]).

In terms of age diversity, OECD survey results for Jordan from 2018 find that around 18% of the ministry's workforce at central level were aged 18-34 years, compared to 26% across the government entities in charge of youth affairs in OECD countries (2019). 43% of MoY's workforce in the youth centres were below 35 years. The relatively low representation of young people in the workforce and professional background of staff working in the youth centres are considered key challenges by MoY. According to the interviews, a significant share of the employees has no university degree or prior experiences in the youth field. Younger (temporary) staff or consultants are primarily recruited through the collaboration with international partners, which raises questions about the sustainability of the workforce planning and accountability (General Budget Department, 2020[18]).

Figure 3.2. Composition of the workforce of Ministry of Youth by job category, 2017-20

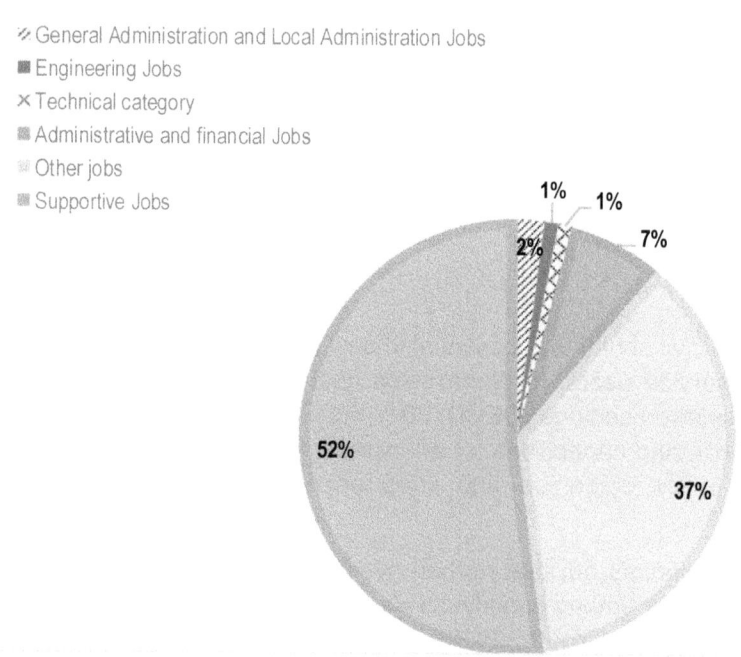

Note: The graph shows the composition of the workforce of the MoY by category in 2020
Source: OECD work based on available information on Draft Budget Law of Government Units for the fiscal and Youth budget of the General Budget Department in Jordan: http://www.gbd.gov.jo/Uploads/Files/gbd/law-gu/2020/en/1.pdf (2020); http://www.gbd.gov.jo/uploads/files/gbd/draft-min/2020/en/3050.pdf (2020 in Arabic)

The Civil Service Bureau (CSB) is in charge of managing employment practices across the public administration in Jordan. Job seekers are invited to submit their application via the CSB website for an open recruitment process that is not linked to a specific position. Applications are examined and reviewed by the CSB once a vacancy in the public sector opens. The selection takes place based on candidates' skills and technical competences (Civil Service Bureau, 2020[19]) (OECD, 2017[17]). Selection criteria include the applicants' graduation year, grade, and experience, which advantages older candidates and has led to the phenomenon of young graduates queuing for public sector jobs. In this regard, in alignment with the results of the 2020 MoY work-life satisfaction survey and the recommendations of the summary report, the OECD Recommendation on Public Service Leadership and Capability holds that the recruitment, selection and promotion processes in public employment systems should be based on merit, transparency, accountability and the rule of law to guarantee fair and equal treatment (OECD, 2019[20]).

Interviews conducted by OECD suggest that workforce planning and management practices in MoY can also be strengthened with regard to the definition of job descriptions. They are considered vague, including for the higher management. Moreover, findings from the interviews suggest that a review of current compensation and performance management could be instrumental to strengthen workforce planning practices and foster a performance system based on merits and adequate incentives.

Incentives and Training for Employees are needed

The Youth Leadership Centre is in charge of running trainings for new staff in the Youth Directorates and youth centres. Available information suggests that the Centre has organised around five courses annually in recent years, which focus on life skills, internal regulations and the objectives of the National Youth Strategy 2019-25. In 2020, the Ministry allocated JOD 9000 to training activities (General Budget Department, 2020[18]). However, there is no training programme in place to build substantive capacities in the field of policy and programme design, implementation and monitoring and evaluation.

The lack of dedicated training programmes in this area tends to sustain a dependency of MoY on its implementing partners in delivering youth-focused programmes and activities.

Important steps have been taken by MoY to understand the parameters driving work-life satisfaction by running an online survey among its employees in 2020 (General Budget Department, 2020[18]). Led by the Institutional Performance Development Unit, the survey is disseminated among MoY staff every two years. Survey replies feed into a summary report that is presented to the Secretary General by. The survey measures staff satisfaction with the working arrangements and internal decision making processes. It also provided an opportunity to evaluate the ministry's performance in regards to internal management, communication, leadership, staff training and development, motivation and incentives, and the working environment.

Based on 366 replies, the results of the 2020 work-life satisfaction survey fed into a summary report, which outlines 15 recommendations to strengthen the internal operations and performance of the ministry[8].

Internship schemes can offer young people the chance to gain skills and experience in public institutions. Governments can also proactively develop their workforce through longer-term, structured graduate programmes aimed at attracting, developing and retaining highly-qualified young talent through training, mentoring, job rotation and accelerated promotion tracks (OECD, 2020[1]). Structured programmes for graduates to join the public sector exist in 42% of the government entities in charge of youth affairs across OECD countries as of 2020 (OECD, 2020[1]). Box 3.1 presents the graduate programmes put in place by Ireland and Australia to attract and develop young talent in the public administration.

Box 3.1. Graduate programmes: Attracting and developing young talent in the public administration

Ireland: Irish Government Economic and Evaluation Service

The Irish Government Economic and Evaluation Service (IGEES) supports an integrated approach to policy formulation and implementation in the civil service based on economic and analytical skills. As a cross-government service, it has provided needed skills and competences to the public administration while attracting and developing the skills of young economics graduates. The recruitment process involves on average 20 graduates per year, with an increase in intake in recent years for a total number of 160 IGEES staff working across the departments as of 2020.

Australia: APS Graduate Programs

The APS Graduate Programs allow new graduates in Australia an entry-level pathway into the public sector. The graduate programs generally take 10 to 18 months to complete, with two to three rotations through different work areas, to give participants a range of skills, knowledge and experience at the start of their career. Participants normally follow face-to-face workshops, trainings and simulation activities. Successful completion of the programs can give participants further opportunities of career development within the public sector as well as study assistance for further training.

Sources: (OECD, 2020[1]) (OECD, 2017[17]).

Financial resources for youth programming are scarce

The budget allocated to the Ministry of Youth has increased by 43% over the last three years to reach JOD 33 million (around USD 46.6 million) in 2020, up from JOD 23 million (around USD 32.4 million) in 2017. This represents an increase inthe share of the central government budget that is allocated to the ministry from 1.4% in 2017 to 2.7% in 2020 (General Budget Department, 2020[18]) (Figure 3.3).

While the share allocated to MoY exceeds the share received by the Ministry of Youth and Sports in Morocco (1.0 %) and the Ministry of Youth and Sports in Tunisia (1.9 %) in 2020 (OECD, Forthcoming[21]), cross-country comparisons must be interpreted with caution as the mandate and responsibilities of each ministry vary. Available information across the OECD countries suggests that, as a share of total government expenditures, the share allocated to the entity in charge of youth affairs makes up less than 1% in most countries (not counting public expenditures on education, among others) (OECD, 2020[1]).

The expenditures of the Ministry of Youth in Jordan are classified according to three categories or "programmes" as per the terminology used by the General Budget Department Report: 1) Administration and Supportive Services; 2) Youth Development; and 3) Sport Development. The highest share of the ministry's budget is allocated to youth affairs (41%), followed by an allocation of 34% to administrative and support services and 25% for sports development (General Budget Department, 2020[18])

Since 2017, the share dedicated to youth programming increased from 31% (General Budget Department, 2020[18]) to 41% or a total of JOD 13.4 million (around USD 18.9 million) in 2020 (General Budget Department, 2020[18]), suggesting a shift towards a greater focus on supporting youth in their transition to an autonomous life.

Figure 3.3. Budget allocation by the Ministry of Youth, Jordan, 2017-20

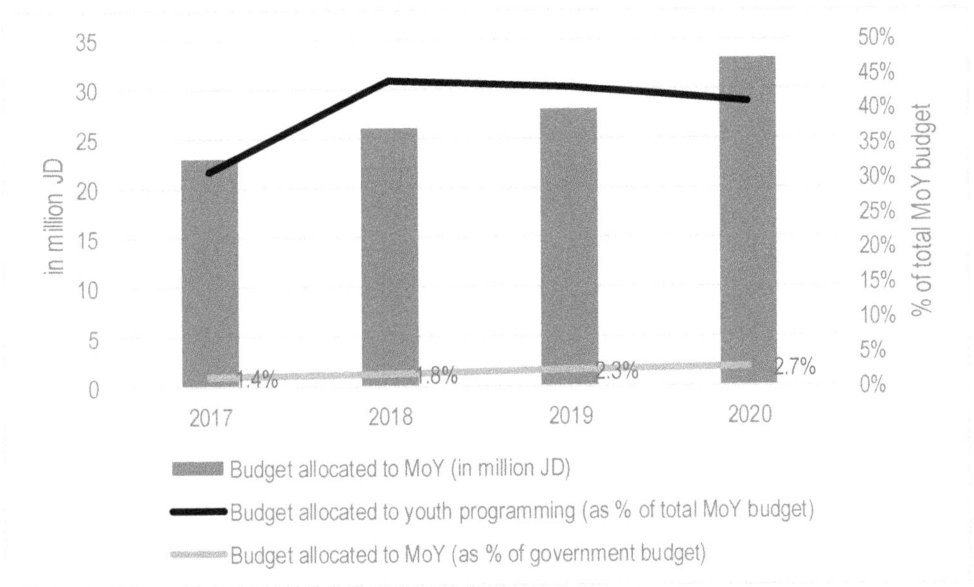

[Chart: Bar chart showing Budget allocated to MoY (in million JD) for 2017 (~23), 2018 (~26), 2019 (~28), 2020 (~33). Black line shows Budget allocated to youth programming (as % of total MoY budget), rising from ~40% in 2017 to ~45% in 2018, then ~42% in 2019 and ~40% in 2020. Light line shows Budget allocated to MoY (as % of government budget): 1.4% (2017), 1.8% (2018), 2.3% (2019), 2.7% (2020).]

Source: (Department, 2018[22]) (General Budget Department, 2020[23]) (OECD, 2017[17]) (General Budget Department, 2020[18])

Only 16 % of the Youth Budget are non-infrastructure costs

The analysis of expenditures in the "Youth Development" category demonstrates that a significant share is spent to maintain and renew the physical infrastructure owned by the ministry. In 2020, 84% of expenditures in this category were dedicated to the establishment and maintenance of playgrounds and sports facilities (JOD 4.4 million equivalent to around USD 6.2 million), the establishment of youth centres and youth houses (JOD 3.7 million equivalent to around USD 5.2 million), and to the management of youth development (JOD 3.2 Million equivalent to around USD 4.5 Million). In turn, as reported by the ministry, around JOD 500,000 (around USD 705,000) have been spent on the implementation of the National Youth Strategy 2019-25 as of May 2021.

Investments into the physical infrastructure are unequally distributed across different governorates. To some extent, this reflects different demographic realities, however, interviews conducted by the OECD also suggest that young people from remote rural areas often find it more difficult to access opportunities provided by MoY. For instance, JOD 1.8 million (around USD 2.5 million) of the total expenditures in the category "playgrounds and sports facilities" were allocated to Amman, which accounts for 42% of the total expenditures in this category (and hosts around 20% of the total population). Similarly, one fourth of the expenditures on "youth centres and youth houses" were invested in Amman, while significantly less than 1% were allocated to the Governorates of Al-Balqa (hosting 5 % of the total population) and Tafileh (hosting 1% of the total population).

From a public governance perspective, it is noteworthy that an estimated JOD 200,000 (around USD 282,000) is allocated to "enhancing the institutional capacities of the Ministry" and JOD 700,000 (around USD 987,000) to "establishing a new building for the Ministry of Youth" in the category "Administration and Support Services". The vast majority (92%) in this category is allocated to current expenditures, including salaries, allowances and promotions, social security contributions, use of goods and services, and subsidies to public institutions (General Budget Department, 2020[18]).

Figure 3.4 displays the capital expenditures (i.e. expenditures allocated to goods and services, buildings and constructions, devices, machinery and equipment, and lands)[9] by the Ministry of Youth across the governorates in 2020. It illustrates that more than one third (35%) of the total capital expenditures were allocated to Amman and Balqa. Further research could analyse the allocation of capital expenditures over time and across governorates in comparison to their respective youth populations in order to identify trends and potential disparities.

Figure 3.4. Capital expenditures by the Ministry of Youth differ significantly across governorates in Jordan, 2020

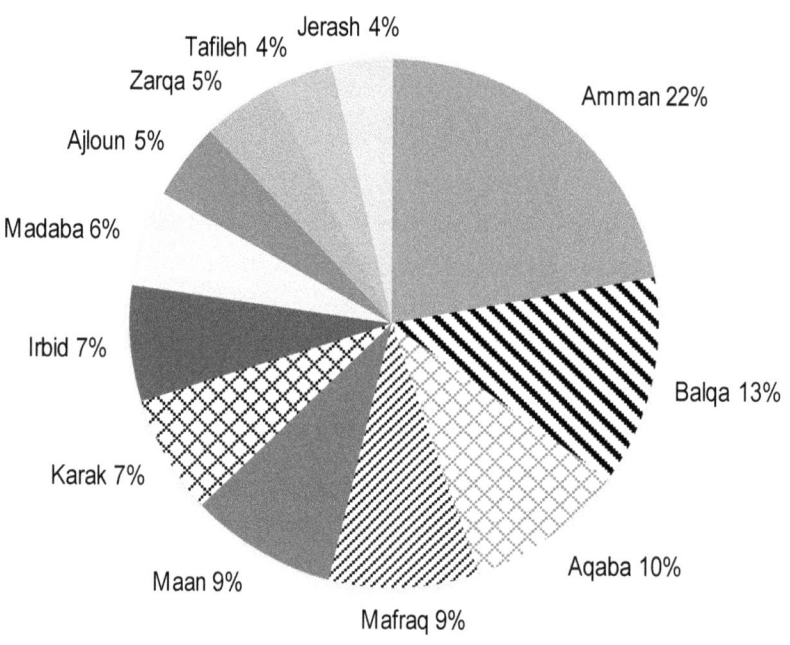

Source: OECD analysis based on available information on Youth budget of the General Budget Department in Jordan, http://www.gbd.gov.jo/uploads/files/gbd/draft-min/2020/en/3050.pdf (p.10).

In terms of current expenditures, the highest share is allocated to salaries and promotions. In 2020, 69% of the total expenditures by the Ministry of Youth were spent on salaries and promotions, decreasing from 77% in 2017 (General Budget Department, 2020[18]).

Figure 3.5. Allocation of current expenditures by the Ministry of Youth in 2017-20

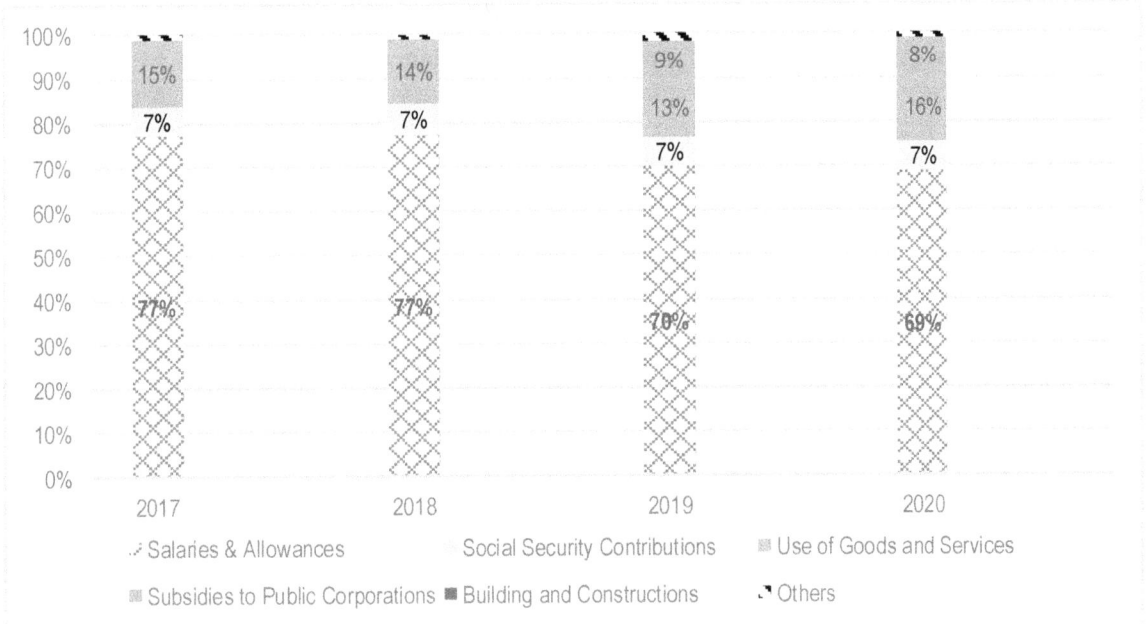

Source: OECD work based on available information on Draft Budget Law of Government Units for the fiscal and Youth budget of the General Budget Department in Jordan: http://www.gbd.gov.jo/uploads/files/gbd/law-min/2019/en/3050.pdf (2019); http://www.gbd.gov.jo/uploads/files/gbd/draft-min/2020/en/3050.pdf (2020 in Arabic).

The availability of comparative data about the resources allocated to "Youth Development" sets Jordan apart from most OECD and MENA countries, in which such information is rarely publicly available. The information is published on an online platform to exchange fiscal data across ministries and departments, which was set up by the General Budget Department within the Ministry of Finance (General Budget Department, 2020[23]).

Coordination across Ministries and Levels of Government

The cross-cutting nature of youth policy requires strong coordination mechanisms across governmental and non-governmental stakeholders. When youth policy and programmes are delivered in a fragmented way, young people find it more difficult to access important services for their transition to an autonomous life. A joint vision and effective co-ordination mechanisms are also critical to unite various stakeholders behind the same strategic and operational objectives based on a clear division of roles and responsibilities (Chapter 2).

Around half of all OECD countries have put in place an institutionalised mechanism for inter-ministerial coordination on youth affairs. As Box 3.2 illustrates, these mechanisms take the form of inter-ministerial or inter-departmental coordination bodies, working groups or focal points (OECD, 2018[14]).

> **Box 3.2. Examples of horizontal co-ordination mechanisms for youth policy**
>
> **Inter-ministerial or inter-departmental co-ordination bodies** are composed of ministries with a responsibility to implement specific commitments of the national youth policy. The ministry with formal responsibility to co-ordinate youth affairs is always part of these structures and usually co-ordinates and prepares its meetings. For instance, Luxembourg set up an inter-department committee for this purpose. It is composed of representatives of the Ministers of Children and Youth, Children, Children's Rights, Foreign Affairs, Local Affairs, Culture, Cooperation and Development, Education, Equal Opportunities, Family, Justice, Housing, Police, Employment, Health and Sports.
>
> **Working groups** are often established on an ad hoc basis and assume responsibility for specific topics. In principle, only ministries with corresponding portfolios are involved in the respective thematic working group. Inter-ministerial co-ordination bodies may be complemented by working groups in which line ministries may take the lead in co-ordinating its activities. In the United States, an Interagency Working Group on Youth Programs supports co-ordinated federal activities in the field of youth.
>
> **Focal points** may be appointed to oversee the work on youth affairs within line ministries and coordinate youth-related programming with the entity in charge of youth affairs. In Slovenia, each Ministry has a dedicated youth focal point to facilitate co-ordination with the Council of the Government of the Republic of Slovenia for Youth (URSM) and other ministries. In Flanders, Belgium, a contact point for youth exists in all agencies and departments.
>
> Source: (OECD, 2020[1])

Putting in place effective coordination mechanisms is particularly relevant in Jordan in which academic institutions, foundations, civil society organisations (CSOs) and community-based organisations (CBOs) fulfil important complementary but often overlapping functions in the youth field.

The National Youth Strategy 2019-25 acknowledges the need for cooperation and coordination between public and private institutions to provide youth with relevant knowledge and skills. The SWOT analysis done by the NYS highlights the need for coordination between public and private institutions working in the youth field (Ministry of Youth, 2019[16]). It also highlights that the objective of encouraging young people's participation in public life shall be pursued alongside the work of official and civil institutions in this area.

As discussed in Chapter 2, the creation of a Steering Committee and Technical Committee to facilitate coordination in the implementation of the NYS 2019-25 marks an important step in this regard. On the other hand, available information suggests that the Steering Committee has not met frequently and that the Technical Committee is still not operational, which risks hampering regular dialogue and coordination among the different stakeholders. To address the coordination challenge, the Ministry of Youth could prioritise the full operationalisation of the two Committees.

Joint initiatives with other ministries are primarily coordinated through a Memorandum of Understanding (MoUs). MoUs are also frequently used by the ministries in charge of youth affairs in Morocco and Tunisia.

Table 3.2. Inter-ministerial coordination in selected MENA countries, 2020

Countries	Institution responsible for horizontal coordination	Departments responsible for horizontal coordination	Main coordination mechanisms
Jordan	Ministry of Youth	None	Memorandum of Understanding (MoU)
Morocco	Ministry of Youth and Sports	Directorate of Youth and Children and Women Affairs; the Directorate of Cooperation, communication and Legal Studies	Memorandum of Understanding (MoU); Institutional coordination bodies and committees; formal meetings
Tunisia	Ministry of Youth and Sports	The General Directorate for Youth; the Ministerial Cabinet	Memorandum of Understanding (MoU); Institutional coordination bodies and committees; formal meetings

Note: The table shows the entities responsible for the horizontal coordination of youth affairs and the main coordination mechanisms used in selected MENA countries.
Source: OECD work based on the replies received from ministries hosting the youth portfolio in Jordan, Morocco and Tunisia.

Practices from across OECD countries demonstrate that strong institutionalised links between the entity with formal responsibility for youth affairs and the Center of Government (CoG) can facilitate political buy-in. In Canada, for instance, until 2019, the Prime Minister also held the position of Minister of Intergovernmental Affairs and Youth. In Austria (Federal Chancellery), Colombia (Presidency of the Republic) and Japan (Cabinet Office), youth affairs continue to being coordinated by the CoG (OECD, 2017[24]). In France, the Director in the department in charge of youth affairs is also the Inter-Ministerial Delegate for Youth and in charge of chairing the meetings of the inter-ministerial committee for youth.[10]

Young government employees can also play a crucial role in fostering inter-ministerial communication and coordination. In the United Arab Emirates (UAE), the Emirates Youth Council (EYC) was created in 2017 to serves as an advisory body for the government and the Minister of Youth on national issues and engagement with governmental and non-governmental stakeholders. The EYC model has been adopted and replicated in six ministries to coordinate youth affairs between ministries and different stakeholders and to supervise the organisation of youth activities and programmes (Federal Youth Authority UAE, 2020[25]) (UAE Cabinet, 2017[26]).

Youth Affairs at the Subnational Level

Effective co-ordination between the central and subnational levels of government is critical to translate the commitments and programmes set out in the National Youth Strategy 2019-25 into concrete programmes and activities on the ground. The first contact young people have with the public administration often takes place at the municipal or district level. The involvement of subnational levels of the government through regular upward (local to central) and downward (central to local) exchanges to inform strategic planning and prioritisation is therefore important.

The respective approach chosen by countries depends on the organisation of the state and determination of administrative and fiscal competencies (e.g. federal vs. unitary), among others. While Jordan is historically highly centralised, the country has undertaken legal and institutional reform efforts in favour of a more decentralised approach. With the adoption of the Decentralisation Law and Municipality Law in 2015, the government articulated the objective of reducing territorial disparities and encouraging a more participatory approach to the identification of local needs and priorities, in particular by establishing new elected councils at the level of governorates (OECD, 2017[17]).

The relationship between the central and subnational levels of government on youth affairs continues to be managed through a deconcentrated approach. Youth Directors represent the Ministry and oversee the work at the level of governorates, including in the youth centres. In reaction to the decentralisation reform, some of the prerogatives of the central level were delegated to Youth Directors in the governorates to facilitate the coordination and implementation of activities at local level according to the interviews[11]. However, their prerogatives continue to be focused on implementing the decisions and directions received by the central level. In addition, the SWOT Analysis conducted as part of the Strategic and Institutional Development Strategy (2021-24) acknowledges that institutional coordination between the central and subnational levels continues to be a challenge[12]. The allocation of financial resources is managed by the central level while certain approval procedures were assigned to the level of the governorates (e.g. signing financial agreements; establishing, moving and renting youth centres in accordance with the existing budgets and approved plans; and approving the maintenance of equipment and buildings related to youth affairs at local level as long as they do not exceed JOD 200). Similarly, certain approval procedures were facilitated in regards to youth clubs and entities, local administration, and youth affairs to facilitate the implementation of activities at local level. For instance, Youth Directors can liaise directly with partners, approve elections of administrative units in youth centres, and appoint trainers. To establish youth clubs, Youth Directors in the governorates require the approval of the central level.

A national dialogue[13] was held in 2019 by the Administrative Committee of the Parliament, in cooperation with the Ministry of Political and Parliamentary Affairs to assess and evaluate the implementation of the decentralisation law. The national dialogue identified the need to ensure better coordination between local actors and ministries and to merge the 2015 Decentralisation Law and Municipality Law into one law to set clear responsibilities between actors at municipal and governorate level. The ensuing draft Local Administration Law was presented by to Parliament in 2020 (OECD, 2017[17]). As highlighted by the OECD report "Engaging Citizens in Jordan's Local Government Needs Assessment Process", the ongoing decentralisation process should "use the new momentum brought about by the new law to revamp initiatives at the local level, in particular to offer new opportunities for participation in the design and delivery of policies and services". The need to improve communication, coordination, and cooperation between the central and local levels of government in order to ensure the effective delivery of services was also highlighted by the COVID-19 crisis (OECD, 2017[17]). This is reflected in the Strategic and Institutional Development Strategy (2021-24), which points out that legislation and manuals should be updated and developed to provide more flexibility and a more decentralised approach at local level[14].

Mainstreaming youth considerations in policy making and service delivery

To mainstream young people's needs in policy making and service delivery, the systematic collection and use of age-disaggregated data, a participatory approach and the definition of youth-specific objectives and indicators across all policy areas are important elements (e.g. employment, education, social policy, housing, etc). Drawing on the 2015 OECD Recommendation on Gender Equality in Public Life (OECD, 2015[27]), youth mainstreaming can be understood as all efforts to assess government action against the specific needs of young women and men from diverse backgrounds to ensure inclusive policy outcomes (OECD, 2020[1]).

Governance tools at the disposal for policy makers to mainstream a "youth" perspective in policy making and service design can take different forms. Young people's engagement in the policy cycle; ex ante impact assessment of the anticipated effects new laws and regulations on youth (e.g. "youth checks"); or the analysis of public expenditure decisions on different groups in society, including youth (OECD, 2017[17]). While the opportunities for youth to participate in public and political life in Jordan will be discussed further in Chapter 5, this section will look at the role of "youth checks" and youth-sensitive budgeting.

Youth checks: Anticipating the impact of regulation on youth

OECD countries are experimenting with innovative governance tools to ensure the responsiveness of policies and services towards the diverse needs of young people. However, despite notable examples, the OECD report "Governance for Youth, Trust and Intergenerational Justice: Fit for all generations?" shows that the use of regulatory impact assessments (RIAs) to support youth-specific goals remains limited. A third of OECD countries use general regulatory impact assessments and provide specific information on the expected impact on youth, whereas 4 OECD countries apply ex ante "youth checks" to consider the impact of new laws and policies on youth more systematically (e.g. Austria, France, Germany and New Zealand). In addition, in Iceland, the Ministry of Education Science and Culture in charge of youth portfolio is in the process of developing a youth check in cooperation with the Office of the Ombudsman for Children (OECD, 2020[1]).

Box 3.3. Youth checks in OECD countries

Established in 2013, **Austria** was the first country to apply a "youth check" at the national level. The youth check provides for an outcome oriented impact assessment on the effects of policy measures on young people aged 0-30. Along five steps (i.e. problem analysis, defining aims, defining measures, impact assessment and internal evaluation), it obliges all ministries to assess the expected effects of each legislative initiative including laws, ordinances, other legal frameworks and major projects, on children and youth.

In **Germany**, the youth check (*Jugendcheck*) acknowledges that the life situation and participation of present and coming youth generations should be considered in all political, legislative and administrative actions of the Federal Ministries. It is considered to be an instrument to support the implementation of the New Youth Policy and a lens through which other relevant strategies (e.g. on demography and sustainability) should be regarded. Along 10-15 questions (e.g. *Does the action increase or alter the participation of young people to social benefits?*) and three central test criteria (e.g. access to resources and possibilities for youth to participate), it anticipates the expected impact of new regulation on young people aged 0-27.

Source: (Jugend für Europa, 2013[28]; OECD, 2020[1])

In Jordan, efforts have been made recently by the government to set up a system for regulatory impact assessments in cooperation with the SIGMA Programme[15]. As a result, in 2020, an impact assessment policy guide was prepared and launched by the Institutional Performance and Policy Development Department at the Prime Minister's Office in cooperation with the Jordanian Institute of Public Administration. The guide aims to build and strengthen the capacities of government institutions and decision-makers on the use and implementation of impact assessment instruments, based on an overview of good practices (MENA FN, 2020[29]).

Youth-sensitive public budgeting

The OECD Recommendation of the Council on Budgetary Governance characterises the public budget as the central policy document of government, showing how annual and multi-annual objectives will be prioritised and achieved (OECD, 2015[30]). It incarnates the contract between citizens and the state, showing how the resources are allocated by the government to turn plans and strategies into programmes, services and support. The allocation of public budgets matter for youth but also for intergenerational justice and the fair distribution of benefits and costs across different age cohorts. When public expenditure decisions are communicated in a transparent way, they can be a powerful tool to restore citizens' trust in government (OECD, 2021[31]).

The OECD Youth Stocktaking Report (2018) describes youth-sensitive budgeting as a way to "integrate a clear youth perspective within the overall context of the budget process, through the use of special processes and analytical tools, with a view to promoting youth-responsive policies" (OECD, 2018[14]). Among the OECD countries, for instance, Canada considers youth-specific objectives in the framework of gender budgeting, including in its COVID-19 Economic Response Plan. In Spain, ministries are required to send a report to the State Secretariat for Budget Expenditures to analyse the childhood, youth and family impact of spending programmes in preparation of the General Budget. The Slovak Council for Budget Responsibility considers intergenerational fairness in connection with the long-term sustainability of public finances (OECD, 2020[1]). The analysis of public investments into children, adolescents and youth recognises that social services and other support structure at an early age do not only benefit individuals but society as a whole.

As demonstrated by some OECD countries, young people can also play an active role in the budget process itself. Governments can apply various innovative methods to disseminate budgetary information and data in a language that young people can understand; moreover, young people can engage directly in the allocation of financial resources (Box 3.4). Efforts to improve youth access to budget information have been undertaken in the last decade in Jordan, resulting in the creation of citizens budgets[16] since 2011[17]. However, it must also be noted that youth attitudes towards participating in the public budget process vary significantly with respect to educational background, family support and existing opportunities to engage. Therefore, additional efforts must be undertaken to ensure that youth from diverse backgrounds can participate in the process, including vulnerable and marginalised groups.

> **Box 3.4. How to involve youth in public budgeting?**
>
> In Portugal, a participatory budgeting initiative was undertaken at the national level in 2017: people aged 14-30 had the chance to elaborate proposals in fields such as sport, social innovation, science education and environmental sustainability for a total amount of EUR 300,000. At the sub-national level, the Portuguese Municipality of Gaia is currently implementing a three-year participatory budgeting initiative dedicated to people aged 13-30 with a total budget of EUR 240,000.
>
> Source: (OECD, 2020[1])

In Jordan, the General Budget Department within the Ministry of Finance makes available on the website of the Ministry: (i) the general budget law approved by the parliament; (ii) detailed budget reports for all government units (including the MoY and Youth Support Fund); and the Citizen Guide to the Budget issued in 2015 (Ministry of Finance, 2021[32]).

With the support of the National Council for Family Affairs and UNICEF, the Government of Jordan implemented a child-friendly budgeting initiative to support the implementation of the UN Convention on the Rights of the Child in Jordan (Chapter 5). In 2009, a child-sensitive budget analysis was conducted for eight ministries covering the ministries of health, education, social development, labour, justice, Islamic affairs, housing and the former Higher Council for Youth. In the first phase of the project in 2009, the

Ministries of Health, Labour, Social Development, and Education were selected to pilot the study and introduce child budgeting into their budgets and to develop Child Budget Engagement Strategies.

The initiative also worked on projections of the medium-term expenditure frameworks to monitor future allocations to child and social protection programmes. It found that spending allocated to children from 2008-2011 remained fairly constant for education, health and labour (93%, 37% and 10% respectively) and increased slightly for Family, Protection and Handicapped Affairs (from 13% to 15%) (National Council for Family Affairs, 2011[33]).

Recommendations

- **Drafting clear job descriptions for each job category** and reviewing the incentive system for employees, introducing transparent performance measures and a merit-based reward system.
- **Setting up a training programme** to strengthen skills and knowledge in policy and programme design, project management, and monitoring and evaluation.
- **Adopting an evidence-based approach to identify the budget needs** of different youth directorates and youth centres to address geographical disparities and inclusive access for youth.
- **Strengthening institutional mechanisms and capacities for coordination** across ministries and with sub-national authorities and non-governmental stakeholders to deliver effective policies and services for young people.
- **Mainstreaming the concerns of youth in policy making and service delivery** by considering to apply governance tools in the rule making and public budgeting process.

References

Civil Service Bureau (2020), *Homepage*, http://csb-ejob.csb.gov.jo/csb_ejob/security.htm?process=showLogin. [19]

Department, G. (2018), *Budget of the Ministry of Youth*, http://www.gbd.gov.jo/uploads/files/gbd/law-min/2018/en/3050.pdf. [22]

Federal Youth Authority UAE (2020), *Homepage*, https://councils.youth.gov.ae/. [25]

General Budget Department (2020), *Draft Government Units Budgets Law*, http://gbd.gov.jo/en/releases/draft-gu. [23]

General Budget Department, J. (2020), *Budget of Ministry of Youth*, http://www.gbd.gov.jo/uploads/files/gbd/draft-min/2020/en/3050.pdf. [18]

Higher Council for Youth and Sports, P. (2021), *Homepage*, http://hcys.ps/ar/page/%D8%A7%D9%84%D8%A5%D8%AF%D8%A7%D8%B1%D8%A7%D8%AA-%D8%A7%D9%84%D8%B9%D8%A7%D9%85%D8%A9. [9]

Jugend für Europa (2013), *Models and instruments of cross-sectorial youth policy: A comparative survey of 9 countries*, European Peer Learning on Youth Policy, https://www.jugendfuereuropa.de/downloads/4-20-3463/130930_JfE__MKP_Ergebnisse.pdf. [28]

MENA FN (2020), *Jordan- Gov't keen to upgrade public services — PM*, https://menafn.com/1100828067/Jordan-Govt-keen-to-upgrade-public-services-PM. [29]

Ministry of Employment, Y. (2021), *Directions Centrales*, https://mejs.mr/directions-centrales/. [13]

Ministry of Finance, J. (2021), *General Budget Department*, http://gbd.gov.jo/en/releases/law-min. [32]

Ministry of Youth (2019), *Jordan National Youth Strategy 2019-2025*, http://moy.gov.jo/sites/default/files/jordan_national_youth_strategy_2019-2025_english_compressed_1.pdf. [16]

Ministry of Youth and Sports (2021), *Homepage of the Ministry of Youth and Sports, Algeria*, https://www.mjs.gov.dz/index.php/ar/ministere-ar/organisation-ar. [7]

Ministry of Youth and Sports (2021), *Homepage of the Ministry of Youth and Sports, Algeria*, http://www.mjs.gov.dz. [11]

Ministry of Youth and Sports (2021), *Homepage of the Ministry of Youth and Sports, Egypt*, https://www.emys.gov.eg/en. [8]

Ministry of Youth and Sports (2021), *Homepage of the Ministry of Youth and Sports, Iraq*, https://www.moys.gov.iq/ar. [6]

Ministry of Youth and Sports (2021), *Homepage of the Ministry of Youth and Sports, Morocco*, http://www.mjs.gov.ma/fr/content/organisation. [12]

Ministry of Youth and Sports Affairs (2021), *Homepage of the Ministry of Youth and Sports Affairs, Bahrain*, https://www.mys.gov.bh/ar/about/Pages/Organizational-Structure.aspx. [5]

Ministry of Youth, S. (2021), *Ministry of Youth, Sports and Profesional Integration, Tunisia*, http://www.sport.tn/index.php/ar/%D8%A7%D9%84%D9%88%D8%B2%D8%A7%D8%B1%D8%A9/%D8%AA%D9%82%D8%AF%D9%8A%D9%85-%D8%A7%D9%84%D9%88%D8%B2%D8%A7%D8%B1%D8%A9.html. [10]

National Council for Family Affairs (2011), *Child Friendly Budgeting Initiative: Issue No. 1 - Jan 2011*, http://ncfa.org.jo:85/ncfa/sites/default/files/publications/child-friendly-budgeting-initiative-issue-no-1.pdf. [33]

OECD (2021), *Trust in Government*, https://www.oecd.org/gov/trust-in-government.htm. [31]

OECD (2020), *Governance for Youth, Trust and Intergenerational Justice (Fit For All Generations?)*, https://www.oecd-ilibrary.org/docserver/c3e5cb8a-en.pdf?expires=1619963547&id=id&accname=ocid84004878&checksum=2EB2D9C66261D27C493D884F5E18AB69. [1]

OECD (2019), *Recommendation of the Council on Public Service Leadership and Capability*, https://www.oecd.org/gov/pem/recommendation-on-public-service-leadership-and-capability-en.pdf. [20]

OECD (2018), *Youth Stocktaking Report: Engaging and empowering youth in OECD countries - How to bridge the "governance gap"*, http://www.oecd.org/gov/youth-stocktaking-report.pdf. [14]

OECD (2017), *OECD Discussion Paper "Towards a new partnerships between government and youth in Jordan*, https://www.oecd.org/mena/governance/Jordan-discussion-paper-Sept2017-web.pdf. [24]

OECD (2017), *Skills for a High Performing Civil Service*, OECD Public Governance Reviews, OECD Publishing, Paris, https://dx.doi.org/10.1787/9789264280724-en. [17]

OECD (2015), *Recommendation of the Council on Budgetary Governance*, https://www.oecd.org/gov/budgeting/Recommendation-of-the-Council-on-Budgetary-Governance.pdf. [30]

OECD (2015), *Recommendation of the Council on Gender Equality in Public Life*, https://dx.doi.org/10.1787/9789264252820-en. [27]

OECD (Forthcoming), *Morocan and Tunisian Youth Governance Reviews*. [21]

Official Gazette, J. (2016), , https://doc.pm.gov.jo/DocuWare/PlatformRO/WebClient/Client/Document?did=44891&fc=7e6f119f-71f4-4ed3-8023-b6a6db8bcb15&orgId=1&_auth=AD557EEE167C7C09809238446C47C976CB6827D509AC970555280F8C806C097A5652931DF8AAE77061F625E186A41CD6C1EC6BD82D71044E251E60D853B. [15]

Prime Ministry Official Website, J. (2021), *government gazette*, http://www.pm.gov.jo/newspaperSubjects/5517/5517.html. [2]

UAE Cabinet (2017), *News*, https://www.uaecabinet.ae/ar/details/news/uae-cabinet-approves-federal-youth-authority-board. [26]

Youth Policy (2021), *Factsheets*, https://www.youthpolicy.org/factsheets/. [4]

Youth Policy (2021), *Homepage*, https://www.youthpolicy.org/. [3]

Notes

[1] In Jordan, the Ministry of Youth and Sports was created in 1984 before it was replaced by the Higher Council for Youth in 2001. According to the National Youth Strategy 2019-25, the aim of the transformation was "to give a greater role and more flexibility to youth work by developing youth care and development processes". The Ministry of Youth was established in 2016 in response to the directives of King Abdullah II, http://moy.gov.jo/sites/default/files/jordan_national_youth_strategy_2019-2025_english_compressed_1.pdf.

[2] Regulation No. (78) of 2016 on "the administrative organisation of the Ministry of Youth" defines its organisational structure. The Regulation also stipulates the creation ofthe Committee for Planning, Coordination and Follow-up, which assists and advises the Minister in his functions.

[3] The CoG is "the body of group of bodies that provide direct support and advice to Heads of Government and the Council of Minister, or Cabinet". The CoG is mandated "to ensure the consistency and prudency of government decisions and to promote evidence-based, strategic and consistent policies". The CoG can play an important role in generating political will and leadership to pursue a cross-sectorial approach, both horizontally, across different ministries, and vertically, across different levels of government, https://www.oecd-ilibrary.org/docserver/c3e5cb8a-en.pdf?expires=1620037610&id=id&accname=ocid84004878&checksum=BBD881B9FCF73F7B2F0ADE00256552BD.

[4] According to the MoY, the Institutional Performance Development Unit is in charge of strategic planning (e.g. preparing and following up the implementation of the NYS in all its phases and operational action plans); monitoring and evaluation (e.g. on the progress of NYS implementation and action plans on a regular basis, and issue relevant reports; setting standards and mechanisms for performance indicators to measure the performance of the Ministry and its diferent units); administrative and organisational development; and for the development of services and operations.

[5] OECD analysis based on the Strategic and Institutional Development Strategy (2021-24)

[6] Article 5.A of the regulation No. (78) of 2016, which defines the administrative organisation of the Ministry. OECD analysis on available data provided by the Ministry of Youth in Jordan

[7] OECD analysis based on the Strategic and Institutional Development Strategy (2021-24)

[8] As reported by the MoY and the Survey results of 2020, the main recommendations are the following:

- Enhancing transparency, open and merit based processes, and equal opportunities among employees with regard to promotions, annual budget increases, rewards and incentives, trainings, among others;
- Adopting a clear and transparent work mechanism to ensure equal opportunities when hiring employees at the MoY;
- Adopting a clear mechanism to better evaluate the performance of employees and ensure the transparency of the results of the evaluation process;
- Ensuring regular surveys to measure employees' satisfaction;
- Better integrate and involve MoY employees in the development of policies and methodologies related to human resource management;
- Better measuring the effectiveness of designing and implementing trainings and development programs;
- Developing training plans based on needs assessments;
- Ensuring regular communication among employees through regular meetings, especially with senior leadership/management;
- Providing clear employees' job descriptions, which contain the responsibilities, tasks, qualifications and skills required.

[9] MoY total expenditures are devided into capital and current expenditures. Capital expenditures include the expenditures allocated to goods and services, buildings and constructions, devices, machinery and equipment, and lands, while current expenditures include salaries, allowances and promotions, social security contributions, use of goods and services, and subsidies to public institutions.

[10] OECD work based on the official website of the Ministry of National Education, Youth and Sports in France, http://www.jeunes.gouv.fr/ministere/missions-et-organisation/organisation-du-ministere/article/la-direction-de-la-jeunesse-de-l

[11] Based on available data provided by the Ministry of Youth in Jordan. In accordance with the Civil Service Order No. 82 of 2013 and its amendments and the order No. 33 of 2005 and its regulations, the central level delegated by a written statement some of their prerogatives to youth directors to facilitate the coordination and implementation of activities. Youth directors must report back to the central level on their decisions taken.

[12] OECD analysis based on the Strategic and Institutional Development Strategy (2021-24)

[13] 43 sessions were conducted as part of this national dialogue with the participation of 1,568 members of civil society, academia and public institutions from across all governorates.

[14] OECD analysis based on the Strategic and Institutional Development Strategy (2021-24)

[15] The SIGMA Programme is a joint initiative of the OECD and the EU, principally financed by the EU. It supported the formulation of the impact assessment policy guide, and will provide the needed advice and technical support during its implementation.

[16] The citizens' budget is an online document prepared by the government designed to reach and be understood by a large a segment of the population in order to provide citizens with a simplified summary of the budget and enhance their participation in the process.

[17] In Jordan, a citizen guide to the budget in Arabic has been published by the GBD since 2011.

4 Youth participation and representation in public life in Jordan

This chapter discusses how the government of Jordan can strengthen youth participation and representation in public life. Youth trust in public institutions and representation in policy making remain limited in Jordan, with the risk of young people disassociating from public and political life. Governance arrangements, laws, policies and institutions can be leveraged to promote a stronger relationship between youth and public institutions. Based on an assessment of the current situation, ongoing reform initiatives and good practices from MENA and OECD countries, this chapter provides policy recommendations to empower youth in Jordan's public life.

A strong relationship between youth and public institutions

In Jordan, less than 5 in 10 young people trust their government. Indeed, only 43% of people aged 18-29 expressed confidence in their national government in 2018-2019, although this exceeds the average of 32% of young people surveyed in the Arab Barometer across MENA economies.[1] The representation of young people in state institutions also remains limited with a large representation gap of 42 percentage points between the share of members of the House of Representatives under the age of 40 (15%) in 2020[2] and the share of people aged 20-39 in the voting-age population in 2019 (57%).[3] This compares to an average representation gap of 12 percentage points in lower houses of parliament across OECD countries in 2020 (OECD, 2020[1]). At the same time, young people demonstrate agency in the public sphere, participating in the public debate through non-institutionalised channels and contributing to community life through volunteering activities.

The discourse about youth in public life in Jordan has been dominated traditionally by conceptions of young people as a potential risk to stability and security (Milton-Edwards, 2018[2]). However, this discourse fails to acknowledge young people's positive contributions to their communities and their stake in decisions that affect their future, overshadowing the structural challenges that lie at the heart of the relationship between youth and public institutions. In fact, the effectiveness of government policies widely rests on compliance and the sustainability of structural reforms requires long policy timeframes (OECD, 2013[3]). When citizens trust state's institutions, they tend to comply voluntarily with rules to a greater extent and they are more likely to accept short-term sacrifices in exchange of long-term, less tangible benefits (Murphy, 2004[4]). This is significant for young people, who will bear most of the long-term consequences of today's decisions. Promoting trust and strengthening the relationship between youth and public institutions is hence crucial to ensure the readiness and resilience of societies to future shocks.

The positive role that young people's participation can have is recognised in the National Youth Strategy (NYS) of Jordan for 2019-2025, which includes strategic objectives on the empowerment of youth in the political, social and economic field, along with the promotion of youth engagement, effective citizenship and leadership. Promoting youth participation and representation in decision-making is particularly important in the face of cultural norms and perceptions that perpetuate a view of young people as lacking experience, skills and interest to be involved in public life.

This chapter:

1. analyses data and trends in youth participation, representation and engagement in the decision-making process;
2. discusses governance challenges that hinder youth relationship with public institutions and how Jordan can address them; and
3. highlights the role of youth work and youth volunteering in promoting resilient societies and how Jordan can strengthen these fields through specific programmes and resources.

Youth express higher trust in government than other age cohorts but less than in the past

Youth trust in the Jordanian government exceeds the trust expressed by other age groups. Indeed, while 43% of people aged 15-29 surveyed in the Arab Barometer Wave V in 2018-2019 expressed trust in their government, only 36% of people aged 30-49 and 37% of people aged 50+ did so. At the same time, youth trust in government has severely deteriorated since 2007, when it stood at 60%.[4] Similar trends have also been experienced across OECD countries, where inequalities in income and opportunities, unemployment and job insecurity, lack of economic growth, perceived corruption and global challenges have undermined youth confidence in public institutions (OECD, 2017[5]; OECD, 2020[1]).

Among the various public institutions, young people in Jordan largely trust the armed forces, the police and the justice system, whereas they express much more limited trust in the public administration and political institutions such as government, parliament and political parties (Figure 4.1). These differences reflect long-term trends and perceptions of the representativeness and effectiveness of different public institutions in Jordan (Kayyali, 2020[6]).

Figure 4.1. Youth trust the armed forces and the police more than political institutions in Jordan

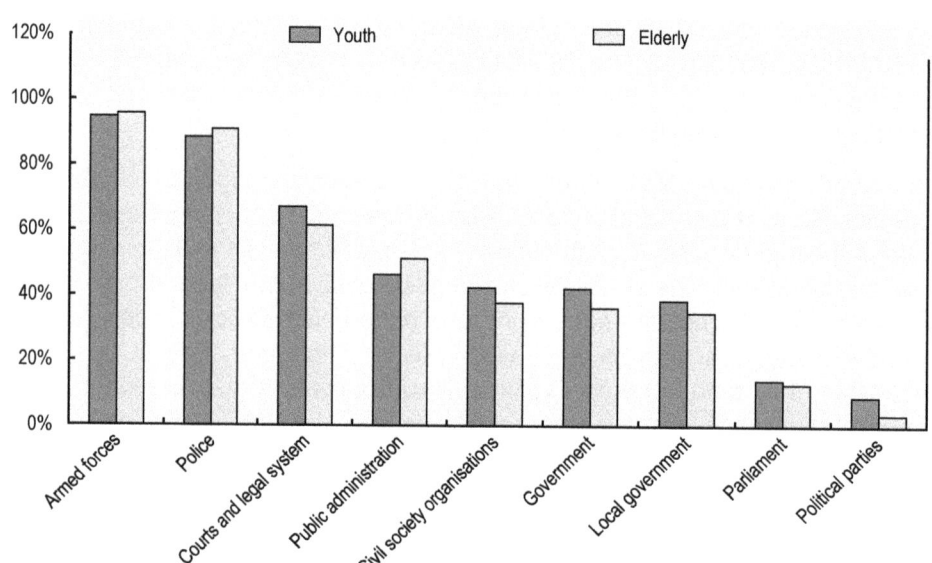

Note: "Youth" are defined here as people aged 15-29 for the question on trust in government and as people aged 18-29 for the questions on trust in all other public institutions; "elderly" are defined here as people aged 50+.
Source: Arab Barometer Wave V.

Trust in public institutions is a multifaceted concept driven by a variety of factors. OECD analysis (OECD, 2017[5]) suggests that governments can promote public trust by delivering services and policies that are high in quality, responsive to citizens' demands, reliable and guided by principles of integrity, openness and fairness. For instance, 48% of people aged 18-29 in Jordan surveyed in the Arab Barometer Wave V in 2018-2019 identify democracy with a government ensuring job opportunities for all. In turn, only 20% of youth in Jordan are satisfied with the government's performance in creating job opportunities, which might hence drive dissatisfaction with public institutions more generally. Furthermore, the perceived level of corruption in the political system also has a significant, negative impact on citizen's trust in public institutions (Rothstein, 2011[7]). In fact, 90% of young people in Jordan think corruption is present at a large or medium extent in their country.[5] Jordan ranked 60th among 180 countries, and 6th among 18 countries in the MENA region in the 2020 Corruption Perception Index by Transparency International.[6]

Chapter 2 has explored the role that National Youth Strategies (NYS) play in supporting young people transition to an autonomous life. Jordan's NYS 2019-2025 also features commitments to reinforce the relationship between youth and public institutions. For instance, it outlines projects and related key performance indicators to promote citizenship education, engagement without discrimination, youth civil and political engagement, volunteering and youth work, among others. Similar areas are also covered in the National Youth Strategies of most OECD countries: the National Youth Strategy of Slovenia (2013-2022) includes objectives and measurable indicators on youth participation in elections as voters and candidates as well as their representation in institutions both at the local and national level. OECD (2020[1]) finds a tendency between the quality of a National Youth Strategy and greater interest of young cohorts in politics across OECD countries. Although the relationship is statistically imprecise, it highlights that investments into the quality of National Youth Strategies and opportunities for youth to participate in public life can be mutually reinforcing.

Promoting an enabling environment for youth participation

Youth engagement and representation do not take place in a vacuum but rely on an enabling environment. Promoting an enabling environment – in terms of legal, policy, institutional, and practical conditions necessary for non-governmental actors to access information, express themselves, associate, organise, and participate in public life – is an important condition for youth to meaningfully participate in public life. Research has also shown that promoting civic freedoms can lead to better societal outcomes, for instance in terms of economic growth and human development (Hogg and Hoodess, 2018[8]).

Jordan was the first country in the MENA region to enact the right to information in 2007, it was the first Arab country to join the Open Government Partnership in 2012, and it has embarked on important decentralisation reforms since 2015, pioneering new initiatives to improve transparency, accountability and participation at the national and local levels. At the same time, important challenges persist in the promotion of an enabling environment for youth participation. OECD analysis shows that significant variations still exist among OECD countries as well when it comes to political rights and civil liberties (OECD, 2018[9]).

In order to engage them as active stakeholders, young people need to have access to information (ATI) and public data to understand and participate in policy-making as well as access to participation opportunities. A recent comparative report published by the OECD finds that Jordan's legal framework on the right to information presents limits due to its vagueness (OECD, 2019[10]). Furthermore, access to information requires governments to have the capacities to respond to ATI requests and pro-actively publish relevant data and information.

Access to information and citizens engagement can also be strengthened through efforts on ensuring open data, which must be pertinent, precise, communicated well and in a timely manner, easy to understand, accessible and easy to use. At the same time, data protection and privacy regulations should be upheld and complemented by an ethical handling of data. The OECD Good Practice Principles for Data Ethics in the Public Sector (2021[11]) can support public officials in the implementation of data ethics in digital government such that public integrity and trust are upheld.

An enabling environment also requires that all people are able to freely express themselves in public, without harassment or retribution, to come together in peaceful protest, and to form or join in associations, groups, movements and civil society organisations. According to 2018-2019 survey data from the Arab Barometer, 44% of youth in Jordan report that freedom of expression is not guaranteed, while 53% stress that their freedom to protest peacefully is not guaranteed.[7] Long administrative approval processes to organise events, vetting processes in the selection of topics, and lack of resources can also represent important barriers according to the interviews conducted by OECD.[8] Similarly, interviews conducted by OECD with youth-led civil society organisations suggest that young people interested in establishing clubs or youth bodies can face tight licensing requirements. Among others, the ministry of youth could consider lowering the minimum age and easing the licensing procedures needed to establish clubs and youth bodies. As further explored in the rest of the chapter, developing opportunities, structures and innovative formats for youth engagement, especially targeting under-represented and marginalised youth, can also be instrumental in creating an enabling environment for youth participation in public life.

Media and digital rights and freedoms are also particularly relevant for young people, as they tend to use digital tools to inform and express themselves, communicate, and associate more regularly than older age cohorts do. Such rights and freedoms are also fundamentally based on the freedom of the press more widely. Data from the Arab Barometer 2018-2019 shows that on average 61% of people aged 18-30 spent 5 or more hours per day on social media across MENA economies, compared to 34% among those aged

30+. Social media are also the primary source of information for 63% of youth in Jordan, compared to 37% of older people, thereby increasing their likelihood of being exposed to misinformation. According to a recent study, for instance, social media accounted for 88% of misinformation related to the COVID-19 pandemic between January and March 2020 (Brennen, 2020[12]). However, the COVID-19 crisis has also revealed vulnerabilities in terms of young people's access to online tools. For instance, more than one in five 15-year olds from socio-economically disadvantaged schools does not have access to a computer for schoolwork across OECD countries (OECD, 2020[13]). In Jordan, only 37% of adults have access to a working computer or tablet at home (Silver et al., 2019[14]). Policies and programmes to ensure more inclusive access to electronic devices, civic digital capability, and connectivity among young users and to protect an enabling environment for youth participation online are critical to overcoming the digital divide and countering misinformation.

Government efforts to combat mis- and dis-information, especially on social media, require whole-of-government approaches, setting clar mandates, promoting coordination across stakeholders, and ensuring sufficient human and financial capacities (Matasick, Alfonsi and Bellantoni, 2020[15]). For instance, in 2018, the Government of Jordan launched the electronic platform "Haggak Tiraf" ("You have the right to know") to combat misinformation.[9] The platform, managed by a specialised team in the Ministry of State for Media Affairs under the Prime Minister Office, monitors and verifies information to provide transparent, accurate and quick information to combat fake news. To fully leverage the potential of this platform, however, the government of Jordan could equip the platform with a clearer classification of the risks posed by a particular piece of misinformation as well as with the necessary human, financial and technical capacities to ensure rapid responses (OECD, 2021 forthcoming[16]). The govenrment of Jordan has also taken action to promote media and information literacy targeting young people through its National Executive Plan on Media and Information Literacy (2020-2023). Strategies, guides, and practical toolkits for countering dis- and mis-information could further strengthen these efforts. At the same time, measures to counter misinformation, hate speech and libel online should be clearly and transparently defined, so as to avoid abuses of discretionary power that might endanger online participation. A debate on balancing these different elements emerged, for instance, during the legislative process of the 2019 Cybersecurity Law of Jordan (Araz, 2020[17]).

Numerous countries have established a children or youth ombudsperson to further institutionalise the protection of the rights of children and young people. While competencies and powers vary widely across countries, 19 OECD countries have created a specific ombudsperson for youth or children at the regional or national/federal level to protect and promote the rights of children and youth, and hold governments accountable. Moreover, 11 OECD countries have created an office dedicated to children or youth within the national ombudsperson office, or included youth affairs as part of its mandate (OECD, 2018[9]). In Jordan, the Integrity and Anti-Corruption Commission was established in 2016 to combat and prevent financial and administrative corruption. Through a memorandum of understanding, the Commission and the Ministry of Youth conduct activities to raise awareness about corruption among young people. The Commission could be further strengthened in terms of mandate, powers and financial and human capacities when it comes to the protection and promotion of an enabling environment for youth participation.

Developing new formats for youth non-institutionalised participation

As of November 2019, only 36% of respondents in Jordan believed that ordinary people can influence decision-making (IRI, 2020[18]). Furthermore, among these, 52% believed protest is the best channel to influence decisions, compared to 23% of them pointing to voting in elections. Available data suggests that young people are more likely to take part in peaceful public demonstrations than older people in Jordan.[10] The preference of young people for non-institutionalised channels over institutionalised channels to exercise civic engagement and participate in political life has also been recognised as a trend across OECD countries (OECD, 2020[1]).

Young people can have numerous reasons to prefer non-institutionalised channels, including notably a lack of confidence in the impact of their participation in institutionalised channels such as elections, lower transaction costs and issue-specific mobilisation (OECD, 2020[1]). Youth participation in non-institutionalised channels also demonstrates their interest and determination in tackling public issues. At the same time, non-institutionalised channels show limitations with concerns around issues of transparency, accountability and unequal access across society (such as by education level, gender, and socio-economic background).

In the last decade, governments at all levels have been increasingly adopting innovative deliberative processes, such as Citizens' Assemblies, Juries and Panels that bring together groups of randomly selected participants and facilitate deliberation to complement the decision-making process of public institutions (OECD, 2020[19]). These mechanisms allow involving citizens more directly in the resolution of issues of major interest from local issues to global ones, such as climate change.

In Jordan, the National Renaissance Plan 2019-2020 recognises the important role of youth in the successful implementation of decentralisation and it seeks to systematically integrate youth in participatory processes for citizens to identify priorities for public services and development objectives at the local level (OECD, 2020[20]). In the Jordanian municipality of Deir Alla, for instance, the decision of where to build a school was prepared in collaboration with a voluntary committee, which featured representatives from the local community (OECD, 2017[21]). However, efforts to ensure the participation of young people in such bottom-up processes remains limited and these processes remain largely at the local level and are not institutionalised in Jordan (OECD, 2020[20]). In France, for instance, the Citizen Convention for Climate brought together 150 citizens, including 14% aged 16-24, in 2019-2020 to discuss actionable measures to tackle climate change.[11] The discussions led to the elaboration of 149 proposals to the President of the French Republic, some of which have informed or fed into the new law tackling climate change passed in May 2021.

Representative deliberative mechanisms provide innovative formats that governments can adopt and adapt to enhance youth participation in decision-making, in coherence and complementarity with the other institutionalised channels. At the same time, the increasing use of these channels by young people demonstrates the need to strengthen institutionalised channels in parallel.

Encouraging young people to go to the ballot box

Voters under 30 years of age represented 38% of the people who participated in the 2020 parliamentary elections in Jordan (Rased, 2020[22]): in 2016, 35% of those who voted were below the age of 30 (European Union Election Observation Mission, 2016[23]). However, the 2020 parliamentary elections also recorded the lowest turnout in more than a decade, with only 29.9% of eligible voters casting their ballot, down from 36% in 2016 (Ma'ayeh and Sweis, 2021[24]). While the share of young people in the citizens that voted may have increased, this might also be due to a contraction of elder citizens' participation, notably due to the sanitary conditions linked to holding elections during the COVID-19 pandemic.

When looking back at the pre-COVID 2016 parliamentary election, survey data from the Arab Barometer Wave V shows that young people participated less than older fellow citizens did. Indeed, 41% of surveyed people aged 18-29 reported having voted in the 2016 parliamentary election, while 55% of people aged above 30 did so.[12] While young people in Jordan reported the third highest participation in elections in the MENA region after Iraq (53%) and Lebanon (42%),[13] their participation rate remains below the average 68% youth's reported turnout across OECD countries among those aged 15-24 for which data exists (OECD, 2020[25]).

Youth participation in elections is affected by a variety of factors, including interest in politics: in fact, with the fourth highest rate across MENA, 52% of young people in Jordan surveyed in the Arab Barometer V reported they are not interested in politics at all, compared to 46% of people in Jordan aged 50+. This compares to an average 24% of young people not interested at all in politics across OECD countries (Figure 4.2). Participation in elections can also be hampered by a lack of confidence in the impact of voting in changing the country's policies and direction and, in some cases, due to fears of negative consequences of becoming engaged in political activities. Electoral disengagement may also be a form of protest in itself. Furthermore, in Jordan, nearly 40% of youth surveyed in a study prior to the 2020 elections reported their tribal affiliation influences their voting behaviour (Ma'ayeh and Sweis, 2021[24]). From a governance perspective, voter registration rules, voting age requirements and civic education are some of the elements that can influence the likeliness of young people to vote.

Figure 4.2. A majority of youth in Jordan is not interested in politics at all, comparison across the MENA region

Percentage of respondents reporting they are not interested at all in politics, by age, 2018-2019.

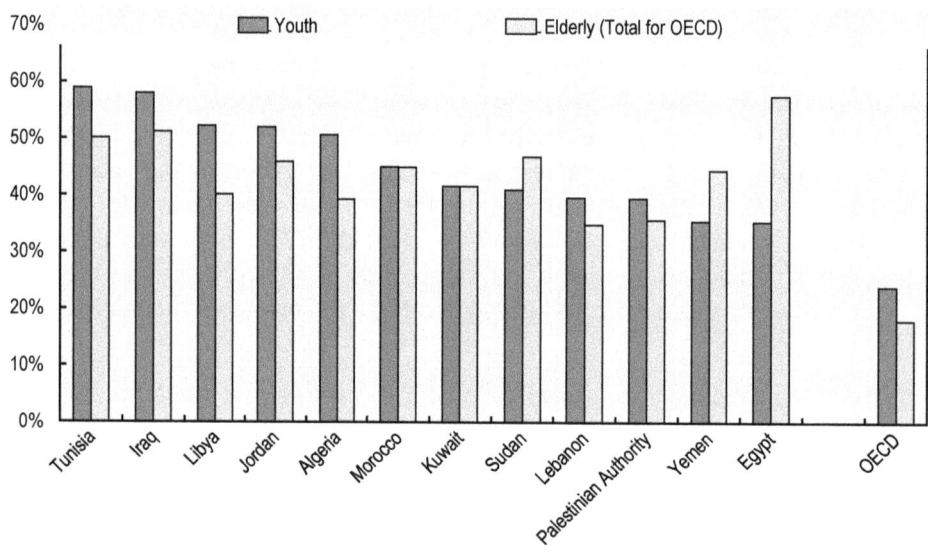

Note: "Youth" is defined here as people aged 19-29 for MENA region and as people aged 15-29 for OECD average. They grey bars refer to people aged 50+ for MENA region and to the total population for OECD average.
Source: Arab Barometer Wave V and OECD (2019), *Society at a Glance 2019: OECD Social Indicators*, OECD Publishing.

Voter registration requirements can represent a considerable challenge especially for first-time voters who are more likely to be changing residency at a time of transition. Governments can take various steps in order to facilitate youth's registration, for instance through automatic registration. Jordan has undertaken steps to facilitate voter's registration. The 2010 electoral law, for instance, initially included fees for registering to vote, which were later removed (National Democratic Institute, 2015[26]). With the 2012 electoral law, citizens needed to present their national identity card and a voter card to vote at the polling station: people were required to register in person to receive the voter card (National Democratic Institute, 2015[26]). Since 2016, the Independent Election Commission became responsible for managing the voter registration, automatically drawing from the civil registry, which is updated by the Civil Status and Passports Department under the Ministry of Interior. Furthermore, national identification card became the unique document for voting: these changes led to the inclusion of some 82% more voters compared to the 2013 election (European Union Election Observation Mission, 2016[23]).

Governments should ensure that young citizens have accessible information at hand on how to register and vote, for instance through information and registration campaigns in schools, universities and other places where young people socialise. Social media can also be leveraged, for example by prominently displaying reliable information and links to governmental websites to all users of voting age.

Voting age requirements can also represent a barrier to the political socialisation of young people. As further explored in Chapter 5, the minimum age required to vote in Jordan is 18 years, although citizens can be added to the voter list already at 17 years 90 days. OECD countries with a voting age below 18 years point to the political socialisation effects by family members and positive impact of school-based voter education programmes for youth aged 16-17 years old to encourage young people to vote. For instance, Austria adopted a general voting age of 16 years in 2007 (OECD, 2020[1]).

Civic and citizenship education can help promote participation

Civic and citizenship education[14] in schools and through extra-curricular activities can be critical enablers of young people's participation in elections as well as more widely in democratic processes and engagement platforms. The 2017 OECD Recommendation of the Council on Public Integrity (OECD, 2017[27]) acknowledges the importance of "carrying out, where appropriate, campaigns to promote civic education on public integrity, among individuals and particularly in schools". This resonates with findings from a recent OECD report "Education for Integrity: Teaching on anticorruption, values and the rule of law" (OECD, 2018[28]) that educating children and youth in the field of integrity and anti-corruption will likely have a positive impact on future civic behaviour.

Civic and citizenship education support youth in understanding and exercising their rights, embrace democratic values, gain awareness of civic and political issues, and acquire the skills to communicate, think critically and engage in decision making (Manning and Edwards, 2014[29]). Civic and citizenship education should not be merely a theoretical exercise and limited to discussions in classrooms. The participation of students in school governance (e.g. student councils), community service and in extra-curricular activities provide spaces to apply theoretical knowledge in practice. Support structures, such as training schemes and funding programmes, are crucial to create an environment in which civic and citizenship education can flourish.

In Jordan, civic education is taught once a week as part of the educational curriculum to Grades 5-10 students, aiming to develop good citizenship among students and to strengthen the sense of loyalty and belonging to their country and to the Arabic and Islamic nation (UNESCO, 2017[30]). The effectiveness of such curricula is however also dependent on the levels of training of teachers in this field, the framing of "good citizenship" and the extent to which textbook-based civic education is linked with more practical and skills-focused aspects.

Civic and citizenship education can also be promoted effectively outside of schools. For instance, the Finnish National Youth Council Allianssi conducts mock elections simultaneously with national and EU elections in order to introduce to voting those who are too young to take part in the elections.[15] In parallel to the 2019 Finnish parliamentary elections, more than 600 schools and 60,000 students took part in such mock elections. Similar initiatives also take place in Jordan with the support of international organisations and donors. For instance, in 2017, the OECD organised mock elections in Madaba involving 23 young candidates and 2,251 young voters ahead of local elections, in cooperation with the RASED Programme of Al Hayat Center for Civil Society Development, the French Embassy and the Independent Election Commission (IEC).[16] More recently, the European Union, in collaboration with the IEC and the Spanish Agency for International Development, organised mock elections with 600 young people from Amman ahead of the 2020 parliamentary elections.[17]

In Jordan, the National Youth Strategy for 2019-25 targets to increase the number of youth workshops on democracy and citizenship to 36 workshops per year by 2025, primarily through its local youth centres.

The role of the youth centres is further explored in Chapter 3. Numerous non-governmental organisations and international donors also conduct initiatives and trainings focusing on strengthening citizenship skills such as critical thinking, public speaking, and debating in Jordan, such as the "Ana Usharek" programme (Box 4.1). While these programmes provide valuable support to young people in Jordan, the number of non-governmental initiatives in this field also points to an important gap in the formal education system to be addressed.

> **Box 4.1. Learning and practicing democratic governance**
>
> **"Ana Usharek" ("I Participate")**
>
> Since 2013, the Programme organised by the National Democratic Institute (NDI) supports young people apply democratic methods and engage in community action. It targets university students in dialogue and debates to learn among youth as well as with politicians about democratic practices and principles, political and electoral systems, local and national governance, human rights, positive communication, citizenship, and gender. Participants of the programme also competed in national debates about current political events in Jordan some of which were broadcasted on national television.
>
> As of May 2021, the programme cooperates with 23 universities throughout Jordan. In the face of the COVID-19 crisis, the programme conducted a social media campaign to encourage students to continue to attend. In less than a week, 1,362 students had joined online sessions across 17 universities.
>
> In 2015, in collaboration with Queen Rania Foundation schools initiative and the Ministry of Education, the Ana Usharek Schools programme was initiated to incorporate the themes addressed in the programme into a civic education programme for middle and high school students, with curricula and manuals to help teachers design and deliver classes. As of June 2021, over 10,500 students from 350 schools have participated in these classes.
>
> Source: https://www.ndi.org/Youth_Political_Participation_Jordan; https://www.ndi.org/our-stories/midst-covid19-ana-usharek-program-goes-virtual; https://www.youthpower.org/innovations/ana-usharek-i-participate-civic-engagement.

Youth remain under-represented in Jordanian public institutions

Promoting a fair representation of young people in public institutions, including the public administration, parliament and cabinet, is critical to ensure that public decisions take into account different perspectives; that policy solutions benefit from a range of experiences and skills; and that policy outcomes are sustainable and responsive to all citizens (OECD, 2020[1]). For instance, OECD quantitative analysis shows that there is a mild tendency between having a higher share of young parliamentarians and young people expressing more interest in politics, although the relationship is statistically imprecise (OECD, 2020[1]).

Youth and the public administration

The public sector has traditionally been one of the largest employers in Jordan: in 2018, the public sector employed 30% of the labour force.[18] More specifically, as of 2018, government employees across public institutions, ministries and authorities represented 23% of the labour force in Jordan.[19] Relatively higher wages, social protection entitlements and lack of opportunities in the private sector have for long made the public sector a favoured choice for young people entering the labour market, especially young women (ILO, 2012[31]). Reportedly, the country's Civil Service Bureau, which handles applications for government jobs, has an employment waiting list that for many positions now exceeds 10 years (Luck, 2019[32]). According to data from the Civil Service Bureau, 392,951 people applied for government employment in 2020, 62% of which were women. Furthermore, 66% of applicants were aged 20-24 and 26% of them were aged 25-29. In 2020, 8031 people were appointed in the civil service following applications in 2019. While age-disaggregated data for new appointees is not available, for instance, 18% of the employees of Jordan's Ministry of Youth were aged 18-34 as of 2018, compared to 26% on average across entities in charge of youth affairs in OECD countries in 2019 (OECD, 2020[1]). Chapter 3 discusses in further detail the human capacities of Jordan's Ministry of Youth.

Jordan's National Employment Strategy 2011-2020[20] identified curtailing public sector employment as one of its priorities. While efforts should be made for the public administration not be identified as the only viable option for young people seeking employment, ensuring a fair representation of youth in the civil service remains instrumental. Indeed, while public administrations with a limited number of young employees do not necessarily fare worse than others in delivering on youth's needs, the OECD Recommendation of the Council on Public Service Leadership and Capability (2019[33]) highlights that governments should build an inclusive and safe public service that reflects the diversity of society, which also includes age-diversity. Furthermore, attracting young people into the public administration can bring new and diverse skill-sets needed for modern public service capability, as well as conduct to better policy outcomes as far as diversity in decision-making can help generate innovative ideas.

Jordan's government can re-imagine recruitment strategies and selection tools to modernise its selection process. Internship schemes can be helpful in offering young people the chance to gain skills and exposure to public institutions: Jordan's public institutions do not run internship schemes, while for instance 62% of OECD entities in charge of youth affairs do so (OECD, 2020[1]). More flexible contractual modalities and dedicated programmes such as graduate programmes can help develop government's workforce by attracting, developing and retaining highly qualified young talent through training, mentoring, job rotation and accelerated promotion tracks. Such programmes, such as the United Kingdom's Civil Service Fast Stream (Box 4.2), exist in 42% of OECD countries (OECD, 2020[1]). Furthermore, as older officials approach retirement, Jordan could mitigate the risk of losing institutional knowledge and experience by developing structured, regular and extensive opportunities for inter-generational learning between older and younger civil servants. For instance, internal secondments, job rotations, networking opportunities, and mentorship programmes can be designed as to promote inter-generational learning in the public administration.

Box 4.2. Developing young talent in the civil service

United Kingdom: Civil Service Fast Stream

The UK Fast Stream is the Civil Service's flagship leadership development programme, recruiting and developing young talent through fast-track training and promotion. Graduates are centrally recruited through a variety of assessments including online tests, work based scenarios, video interviews, group exercises, and panel interviews. There are 15 different schemes on the Fast Stream, each offering a career path toward a government profession, from generalist ones to professions focused on digital and data, finance, economics, science and more. The Fast Stream schemes, lasting between 2 and 4 years, expose the recruited young people to placements in different departments and authorities, a variety of roles, as well as dedicated networking, learning and development opportunities. Upon successful completion of the scheme, participants to the Fast Stream are integrated in the Civil Service.

Source: https://www.faststream.gov.uk/.

Youth representation in parliament and cabinet remains limited

According to data from the Inter-Parliamentary Union (IPU), only 12% of the members of Jordan's House of Representatives are under 40 years of age as of May 2021, the lowest share among MENA countries for which data is available and below the OECD average of 22% (Figure 4.3). Furthermore, this compares to the fact that people aged 20-39 in Jordan made up 57% of the voting-age population as of 2019.[21] The resulting representation gap of 42 percentage points stands out as particularly large when compared to the average representation gap of 12 percentage points in lower houses of parliament across OECD countries in 2020 (OECD, 2020[1]). Age-representation gaps are often more pronounced in countries' leaderships: in fact, according to data from the Hayat Center, the average age of Jordan's cabinet members was 59 years as of September 2020 (Hayat Center-Rased, 2020[34]). Similarly, the average age of cabinet members varied between 45 and 62 years across OECD countries, with an average of 53 years as of February 2018 (OECD, 2018[9]).

Figure 4.3. Youth in Jordan remains under-represented in parliament, comparison across MENA region

Share of members of parliaments (MPs) in lower chambers and unicameral parliaments aged 40 or below, 2021

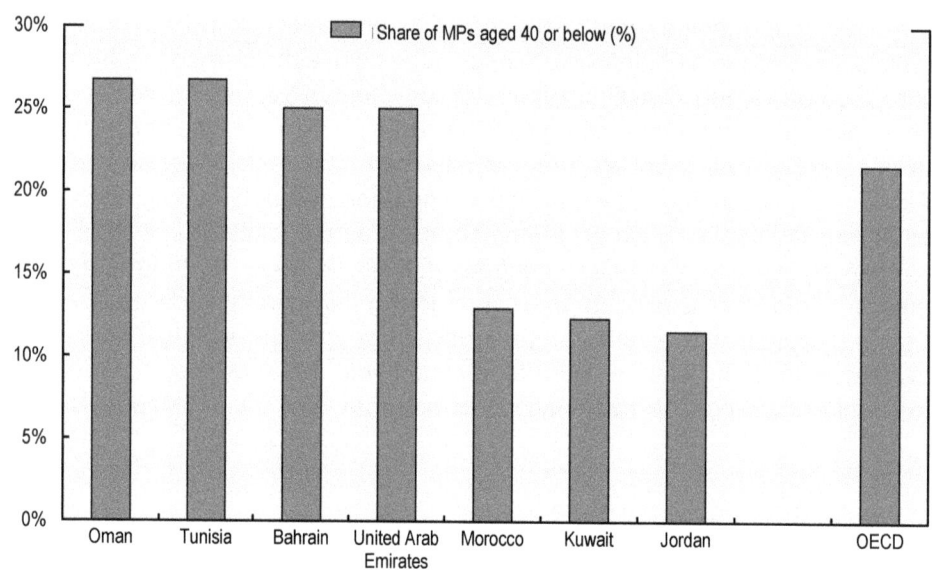

Note: "OECD" refers to the average across 33 OECD countries for which data was available as of 2020.
Source: Inter-Parliamentary Union, *Parline database on national parliaments* (https://data.ipu.org) and (OECD, 2020[1]).

While representative institutions do not necessarily need to mirror the composition of the population, OECD analysis finds a mild tendency between having a higher share of parliamentarians under the age of 40 and young people expressing more interest in politics (as well as feeling more politically empowered), although the relationship is statistically imprecise (OECD, 2020[1]). Furthermore, large representation gaps are a warning sign about norms, rules and regulations that may hamper youth's access to public institutions and limit their aspirations in the first place. For instance, in the 2017 elections for majors and for governorate and local council seats, only 6% of the 6,623 candidates were under the age of 30 and only 14% were under the age of 40 (Milton-Edwards, 2018[2]).

Traditional stereotypes of young people as lacking the necessary experience, financial and legal obstacles, as well as minimum age requirements (Chapter 5) can represent major obstacles for youth who would like to run as candidates in elections. Differently from Jordan, across OECD countries that have a National

Youth Strategy, 38% of them included specific objectives on strengthening youth representation in state institutions (OECD, 2020[1]).

Running a campaign can require investing considerable financial resources and undergoing complex legal procedures. In Jordan, all candidates are required to pay a JOD 500 registration fee (around USD 705) and each list must pay a refundable deposit of JOD 2,000 (around USD 2,820) (Milton-Edwards, 2018[2]). The dominance of personal connections ("wasta") can also represent a barrier to young people's participation in politics given a young persons' presumed limited social capital. In other countries, political parties and their youth wings can offer avenues to reduce such financial and social capital barriers: yet, their role remains limited in Jordan. In the 2020 parliamentary elections, 41 political parties ran for elections, with 389 candidates (i.e. 23% of the total number of the contestants); yet, only 12 party members won a seat in parliament, i.e. 9% of the total number of members of parliament (Ma'ayeh and Sweis, 2021[24]; Kao and Karmel, 2020[35]). According to data from the Arab Barometer Wave V, in 2018, only 9% of youth surveyed expressed trust in political parties in Jordan and less than 1% of them are members of a political party (Kathrin, 2018[36]). Some efforts have been made in this area: for instance, in collaboration with the Ministry of Political and Parliamentary Affairs and the Netherlands Institute for Multiparty Democracy, Jordan's Ministry of Youth launched the Jordan School of Politics (JSoP) in 2019. JSoP is a training programme that aims to encourage youth participation in public life through building trust and democratic values and develop skills and knowledge for young politicians.

As discussed in further detail in Chapter 5, young people need to be at least 30 years old to run as candidates for the national parliament and at least 25 for run in local elections. These thresholds compare to an average age requirement of 20.1 years for lower houses of parliament and unicameral systems across OECD countries and 24.7 for upper houses (OECD, 2020[1]). In 2011, the Royal Constitutional Review Committee issued a recommendation to reduce the candidacy age to 25. Similarly, the EU Election Observation Mission to the 216 elections (2016[23]) recommended to decrease the eligibility age for membership of the Chamber of Deputies to align with existing thresholds for municipal councils. In fact, Stockemer and Sundström (2018[37]) find that for every year candidate age requirements are lowered, the share of young deputies aged 40 and lower increases by more than 1 percentage point.

In Jordan, gender and minority quotas reserve 15 of the 130 parliamentary seats to women and other 15 to minority communities (Christians: 9, Circassians: 3, Chechens: 3). In the 2020 elections, no female candidate won a parliamentary seat beyond the 15 seats reserved to them. A few countries in the MENA region have also adopted youth quotas, including Egypt, Morocco, and Tunisia (IPU, 2018[38]), whose experiences might be interesting for consideration for Jordan as well.

Including youth in the policy cycle

An inclusive policy cycle is crucial to ensure that policy outcomes deliver on the diverse needs of citizens and benefit from their diverse experiences. As recognised in the OECD Recommendation of the Council on Open Government (2017[39]), stakeholder[22] participation in the policy cycle increases government's accountability, broadens citizen's empowerment and influence on decisions, builds civic capacity and improves the evidence for policy-making, among others. For instance, OECD analysis shows that youth organisations that were involved in the policy cycle to a greater extent, also reported higher satisfaction with government's performance across public service areas such as transportation, health, housing and employment among others (OECD, 2020[1]). Ensuring transparency and communication, setting commitments, and taking initiatives for informing, consulting and engaging young people and their organisations are crucial steps to include young people in the policy cycle.

Ensuring youth-targeted communication

Transparency is about ensuring that citizens and other stakeholders can observe, understand and monitor the activities of the government, at the national as well as subnational level. Ensuring access to information and open data are particularly relevant to young people.

Beyond ensuring transparency, an enabling environment for young people to participate in the policy cycle requires effective and youth-targeted communication. For instance, Jordan's National Youth Strategy 2019-25 highlights communication with young people as one of the most important priorities in building and developing the strategy. Most young people in Jordan are growing up as "digital natives" and demonstrate strong awareness and skills in mastering new digital technologies. While this development comes with its challenges (such as the spread of fake news), digitalisation offers new opportunities for young people to participate and engage in public life.

As recognised in the OECD Recommendation of the Council on Open Government (2017[39]), governments should promote innovative ways to promote stakeholder participation by leveraging digital government tools. Jordan's Ministry of Youth has undertaken significant efforts to open up new information and communication channels through its Twitter, Facebook and Instagram profiles since 2016 as well as through weekly newsletters. As of May 2021, the Facebook and Twitter account, which are updated with information about the activities of the Ministry on a daily basis, count more than 141,000 friends and 28,000 followers respectively. Since 2016, the Ministry of Youth also has its own Youtube channel, although it is visited less frequently. The Ministry's website is available in both English and Arabic and provides general information about the ministry, youth cities and sport facilities as well as youth clubs. It features a platform for young people to submit their ideas and initiatives. Moreover, important conferences in the field of innovation in Jordan include the Arab Artificial Intelligence Summit, held in October 2019, and the Innovation Forum, organised with the Minister of Youth in February 2020.

Building on these steps, future efforts could focus on moving gradually from a one-way dissemination of information to a two-way, more regular consultation of youth with the support of digital tools. A range of traditional and digital forms of communication such as online platforms and social media can be leveraged depending on the particular communications objective. Such efforts require policy makers to tailor their messages and delivery modes to the intended audience, on the basis of research into the motivations, fears and barriers faced by young people. The OECD Communication Guide on Engaging Young People in Open Government (OECD, 2018[40]) also highlights the importance of communicating as early as possible, presenting clear and detailed reasons, scope of interaction and expected outcomes. Furthermore, governments can help equip young people with the capacities to engage safely in communication. For instance, within Jordan's National Youth Strategy 2019-25, the Ministry of Youth and other ministries will implement awareness programmes to promote positive uses of social media and "immunise" young people against the dangers of hate speech.

Setting commitments to promote youth participation

Commitments on youth participation in National Youth Strategies and sectoral plans can create stronger mandates, earmark resources and establish monitoring mechanisms across ministerial portfolios and levels of government.

National Youth Strategies most commonly feature objectives and commitments on youth participation in the policy cycle: for instance, this is the case for 75% of OECD countries that have a NYS in place (OECD, 2020[1]). Similarly, Jordan's NYS 2019-25 includes commitments and outlines projects to empower youth in the political, social and economic field, strengthen their engagement in the policy cycle, and promote effective citizenship and leadership.

Sectoral strategies can also be used to set commitments and priorities in this field. For instance, Jordan's Renaissance Plan 2019-20 features commitments to integrate youth in public life and decision making; to develop their democratic culture, citizenship and pluralism; and to review legislation related to increasing the political participation of youth, among others. Similarly, the decentralisation process, which started in Jordan with the adoption of the Decentralisation Law and the Municipality Law in late 2015, has given new impetus to strengthening youth participation at the local level, bringing local authorities closer to citizens and raising hopes of encouraging youth-driven, bottom-up initiatives, greater transparency and accountability. At the same time, OECD analysis highlights a number of barriers limiting the potential impact of decentralisation on citizens' participation, such as the lack of clear roles and responsibilities across levels of government and the lack of resources (OECD, 2017[21]).

As the first Arab country to join the Open Government Partnership (OGP) in 2012, Jordan has pioneered new initiatives to improve youth participation in the broader framework of advancing more open, transparent, participatory and inclusive policy making. For instance, OGP's Jordan End-of-Term Report for 2016-2018[23] identifies that Commitment 5 on conducting training programmes with target groups including youth and on conducting the first-ever governorate council elections had a major, positive impact on allowing strengthening civic participation and opening the government. The Ministry of Political and Parliamentary Affairs was responsible for the trainings and workshops. The 4th OGP National Action Plan of Jordan 2018-20,[24] launched in October 2018, for the first time refers specifically to youth institutions, which shall be included in the national dialogue on reforms (Commitment 3). Including youth-specific commitments in these action plans can be an effective way of promoting youth participation in the policy cycle not only within the Ministry of Youth, but also across ministries and government entities, given their cross-sectorial scope. However, the open government agenda still remains a largely untapped resource in Jordan from a youth perspective. The elaboration of future plans could involve youth already in the design phase to ensure that their concerns inform the elaboration of objectives and commitments.

Engaging young people and their organisations

Engaging youth in the policy cycle goes beyond informing and consulting them. As highlighted by the OECD Recommendation of the Council on Open Government (2017[39]), engaging citizens requires giving them the opportunity as well as the necessary resources (e.g. information, data and digital tools) to collaborate during all phases of the policy and service cycles, from design and implementation, to monitoring and evaluation.

Chapter 2 highlights how young people were consulted in the formulation of Jordan's National Youth Strategy 2019-25 through surveys and focus groups: yet, the consultations largely took place in the review phase when core commitments had already been identified. Furthermore, youth participation should not be limited to the policies and services delivered by the Ministry of Youth. For instance, in Norway, the Ministry of Culture consulted children and young people between the age of 3 and 19 in the formulation of a white paper on art, culture, and digital artistic and cultural expression in 2019.[25]

Public authorities can take targeted steps to ensure the participation of young people in broader citizens' participation channels such as public hearings, consultations, surveys, town hall meetings, and participation to strategic planning. Engaging young people in deciding how public resources are allocated, for instance through participatory budgeting programmes (Box 4.3), can ensure that their interests are addressed in public expenditure and increase their interest and ownership in an exercise otherwise perceived as technical, while also increasing transparency and accountability (OECD, 2020[1]). Such programmes can be particularly useful when young people are involved in the whole process of designing, selecting and implementing the budgeted projects. In Jordan, the Ministry of Municipal Affairs has implemented participatory budgeting programmes in a pilot with three municipalities, with reportedly satisfying results (OECD, 2017[21]). Experiments with participatory budgeting schemes at the subnational level could be replicated and expanded, for instance by establishing formal mechanisms through which young people and their organisations (as well as citizens and CSOs generally) can participate in the budget process.

> **Box 4.3. Participatory budgeting can help bring young people in**
>
> **Sweden: Helsingborg's "Vision Fund"**
>
> Since 2014, the Swedish city of Helsingborg runs a "Vision Fund" to finance citizens' initiatives that will help the city reach its 2025 Vision. Many of these projects are led by young people, although youth are not directly involved in the project selection. The Fund is equipped with approximately USD 120,000 (SEK 1,000,000) per year and each project can receive funding up to approximately USD 12,000 (SEK 100,000) as well as support in the form of coaching and trainings.
>
> **Tunisia: La Marsa's public lighting**
>
> Article 137 of the new Tunisian constitution stipulates that local communities, within the framework of the approved budget, have the freedom of allocating their resources according to the rules of good governance. La Marsa, a coastal community of 110,000 residents, was the first municipality in Tunisia to institute a participatory budgeting programme, with a focus on public lighting.
>
> A series of public meetings were held in each of the five districts within the municipality to explain participatory budgeting, provide an overview of the city budget, and present technical information on lighting services delivery. Participants then divided into small groups to discuss possible projects and priorities, which were then presented to the rest of the participants. All participants were invited to vote by secret ballot on all the proposed projects. The projects and priorities were then presented and voted by districts' delegates in municipal assemblies: as a result, lighting was increased in high crime areas and near schools, as well as in places frequented by women and children. The district delegates were also involved during the implementation stage and maintained communication with their local communities on progress.
>
> Source: https://helsingborg.se/kommun-och-politik/helsingborg-2035/visionsfonden/; (OECD, 2020[41]).

Efforts to engage young people in the policy cycle require adequate financial and human resources, open information, good co-ordination and appropriate incentives for public officials to close the feedback loop. Special attention should also be paid to engaging marginalised youth, for instance holding consultations in different geographical areas away from the capital or reimbursing expenses. Digital tools can also be leveraged to reduce transaction costs for participants, although digital divides across socio-economic groups should be taken into account.

Youth-led organisations and youth representative bodies can play a crucial role in creating bridges between public authorities and young people for instance through initiatives and programmes on youth participation (Box 4.4). National youth councils (exist in 78% of OECD countries) and local youth councils (exist in 88% of OECD countries) also provide important fora for youth participation: for instance, in countries such as Finland and Norway, the establishment of local youth councils is mandatory at the municipal level (OECD, 2020[11]). Furthermore, a majority of OECD countries (53%) have also established youth advisory councils affiliated to specific ministries or to the centre of government. In in Denmark, for instance, the Ministry of Environment and Food has established a Youth Climate Council to advise the Ministry on climate policy. While in Jordan youth councils or youth advisory councils do not exist at the national or local level, the Ministry of Youth has made efforts to establish a "Youth Shadow Government" and a "Youth Shadow Parliament." Such programmes should be equipped with the necessary resources, inclusive membership and clear mandates to ensure they meaningfully engage youth in the policy cycle.

> **Box 4.4. Structured dialogue between youth and municipalities**
>
> **Jordan: I dare for sustainable development**
>
> I dare for sustainable development, a youth-led civil society organisation, led a pilot project in the municipality of Ein-Albasha to institutionalise a structured dialogue between youth and municipalities in 2014. Based on a four-month testing phase, a one-year project was conducted with six municipalities in Great Tafileh, Qadissyeh, Great Ajloun, Kufranjeh, Great Salt and Shouneh with young people aged 18-30 years.
>
> The project aimed at establishing a model for structured dialogue between youth and municipalities. Initiated during the elaboration of the decentralisation law, the project participants deplored a significant lack of knowledge among young people and local authorities as to the future opportunities for young people to engage.
>
> The project resulted in a capacity-building programme, organised jointly for youth and local authorities, to strengthen knowledge, skills and attitudes in areas that were considered crucial to establish a structured dialogue. The programme included modules on the concept of identity and active citizenship, decentralisation and municipality laws, mapping of community/municipality resources and the identification of possible solutions, action plans and a long-term strategy for the municipality.
>
> According to I dare, the project resulted in the establishment of two youth units in the municipalities of Ajloun and Kufranjeh with a dedicated budget. Main challenges were experienced in elaborating tailored programmes for the young people running the units.
>
> Source: https://www.i-dare.org/

In partnership with governments, youth representative bodies with clear mandates, independence, access to decision-making, adequate capacities and an inclusive membership can promote innovative and youth-responsive policy solutions and foster active, democratic citizenship among young people.

Young volunteers: builders of resilience

In the midst of the COVID-19 crisis, youth organisations, youth workers and young volunteers have stepped in, supporting the most vulnerable people and promoting societal resilience (OECD, 2020[42]). In Jordan, for instance, the government provided opportunities for young people to support efforts to limit the spread of the virus by volunteering in the health field and in community awareness and guidance.[26] Chapter 3 further explores the role of Jordan's youth centres in empowering young people and promoting resilient societies and it assesses the challenges and opportunities they face.

Volunteering is a powerful tool for combatting social exclusion, promoting youth's development, consolidating their trust and co-operation, cultivating their civic sense and building societal resilience (OECD, 2020[1]). Yet, (formal) youth volunteering in Jordan remains limited compared to other MENA economies and OECD countries (Figure 4.4). For instance, in Jordan, 11% of people aged 18-29 surveyed by the Arab Barometer in 2018-2019 reported having volunteered for a local group or organisation, compared to 22% of people aged 15-29 reporting having done so across 24 OECD countries in 2019.

Figure 4.4. Youth official volunteering in Jordan remains limited, comparison across MENA region

Share of people aged 18-29 reporting to have volunteered for a local group / organisation, 2018

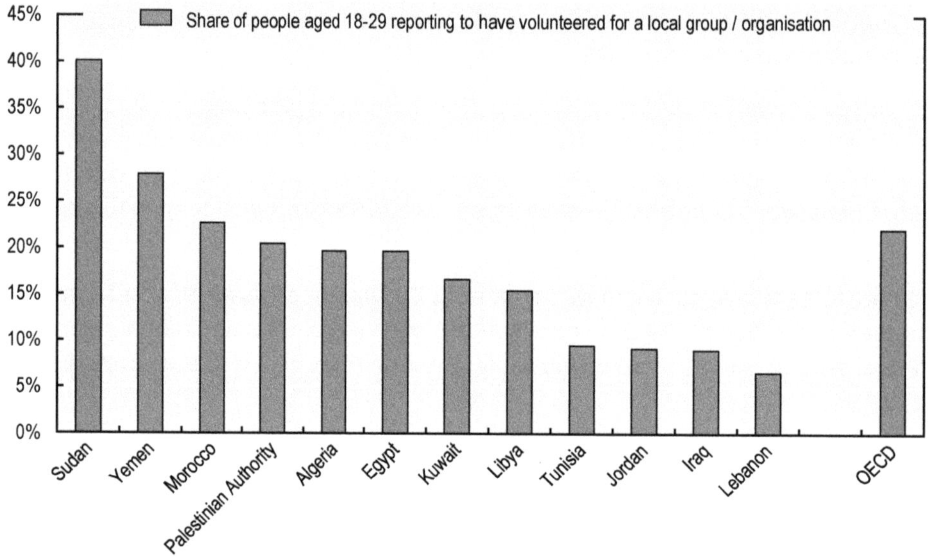

Note: "OECD" refers to the average across 24 OECD countries for which data was available as of 2019.
Source: Arab Barometer Wave V and (OECD, 2020[1]).

Youth volunteering can be hampered by a number of factors including lack of opportunities, resources and awareness and limited co-ordination across stakeholders. Difficulties related to logistics or personal costs can also represent a barrier for young people from disadvantaged backgrounds. These challenges remain common also among OECD countries (OECD, 2020[1]).

Several countries, including Jordan, include strategic objectives on youth volunteering within their National Youth Strategy, which can be useful to clarify responsibilities, create monitoring and accountability mechanisms, and ensure dedicated financial resources. In Jordan, one of the guiding elements of the National Youth Strategy 2019-2025 is the encouragement and promotion of voluntary work. Among others, Jordan's NYS commits the Ministry of Youth, in collaboration with other relevant ministries, foundations and international organisations, to run 24 volunteer initiatives per year for local community service and the school environment, as well as to establish and activate a Bank of Volunteers in Jordan. While a number of volunteering opportunities are provided in Jordan by foundations, CBOs and CSOs, government-led, well-financed, national youth volunteering programmes can be effective in promoting youth volunteering (Box 4.5). In fact, OECD analysis finds a positive and precise relationship between having a national programme for youth volunteering and young people volunteering more compared to the total population (OECD, 2020[1]).

> **Box 4.5. Promoting youth volunteering**
>
> **Jordan: Al Hussein Youth Camps and the Jordanian Youth Commission**
>
> Al Hussein Camps, established in 1961 under the initiative of His Majesty the late King Hussein, seek to provide young people with opportunities to develop their talent through overnight camps including activities on sport, adventure, Internet of Things, artificial intelligence, robotics and social cohesion.
>
> The Jordanian Youth Commission, launched in 2006 by His Majesty King Abdullah II and implemented by the King Abdullah II Fund for Development, aims to strengthen youth's capacities to participate in public life and enhance voluntary work. In particular, through the "We Volunteer for Jordan" programme, the Commission has been implementing more than 133 local volunteering activities with the participation of 6,778 young people from across Jordan's governorates.
>
> **France: Civic Service in Solidarity of the Elderly (Service Civique Solidarité Seniors)**
>
> In March 2021, the French government expanded the existing civic service programme to promote solidarity between young people and the elderly through volunteering work. Since 2010, more than 500,000 people aged 16-25 and people with disabilities aged 16-30 participated to the Civic Service volunteering programme. The new addition focused on the elderly will allow the creation of 10,000 further opportunities for young people to volunteer their time in support of around 300,000 elderly over 3 years. Volunteers receive an allowance of around EUR 473 net per month provided by the State.
>
> Source: https://www.kafd.jo/en/Projectsa.aspx; https://www.jordantimes.com/news/local/al-hussein-youth-camp-kicks-aqaba-myriad-activities; https://www.service-civique.gouv.fr/uploads/content/files/2_dossier_de_presse_sc2s_vf.pdf

Effective co-ordination across stakeholders of the volunteering sector is essential for an effective implementation of national youth volunteering programmes and initiatives. In Jordan, a Higher Committee for Volunteer Work has been established in 2021 by a decision of the Prime Ministry.[27] The Committee is chaired by Jordan's Minister of Youth and it includes the Executive Director of the Crown Prince Foundation and the Secretary Generals of the ministries of labour, culture, social development, youth, the Director of Civil Defence, the Executive Director of the King Abdullah Fund, and pioneers in the volunteer sector. The Higher Committee aims to institutionalise, organise and frame voluntary work in Jordan, ensuring a safe enabling environment in partnership between public and private stakeholders and promoting volunteering especially among young people. Equipping the Higher Committee with the necessary political support, resources, mandate and tools could be instrumental in promoting youth volunteering by creating a coherent and enabling environment and by delivering well-resourced volunteering programmes.

Recommendations

This chapter has analysed the current state of the relationship between young people and public institutions in Jordan across a variety of dimensions, it has assessed government's efforts in promoting youth participation and representation in public life and it has presented innovative practices. While important efforts and advancements have been made to rebuild youth trust in government and strengthen their relationship with public institutions, the government of Jordan could consider:

1. **Protecting and promoting an enabling environment for youth participation** both offline and online as well as for youth-led organisations, reducing the minimum age and easing the licensing procedures needed to establish youth-led organisations.
2. **Exploring the co-creation of innovative mechanisms of stakeholder engagement** targeting young people, in coherence and complementarity with the other institutionalised channels.
3. **Strengthening civic and citizenship curricula** in schools and out-of-school programmes to reinforce youth's association with democratic processes.
4. **Providing dedicated programmes to help talented youth join and thrive in the public sector workforce** and promote inter-generational learning between older and younger employees.
5. **Adopting a government-wide policy on youth engagement in policy and strengthening in-person and digital means**, considering options such as enhanced participatory budgeting programmes and the establishment of youth councils at national and local level as well as youth advisory councils affiliated to specific ministries.
6. **Leveraging the open government agenda to promote youth participation in public life**, including by associating the Ministry of Youth and youth stakeholders more closely with the design and implementation of national action plans for the Open Government Partnership.
7. **Promoting national youth volunteering programmes** and providing political support, resources, mandate and tools to the Higher Committee for Volunteer Work to ensure a coherent and enabling environment for youth volunteering.

References

Araz, S. (2020), *Jordan adopts sweeping cybersecurity legislation*, https://www.mei.edu/publications/jordan-adopts-sweeping-cybersecurity-legislation (accessed on 11 May 2021). [17]

Brennen, S. (2020), "Types, Sources, and Claims of COVID-19 Misinformation", https://reutersinstitute.politics.ox.ac.uk/sites/default/files/2020-04/Brennen%20-%20COVID%2019%20Misinformation%20FINAL%20(3).pdf. [12]

European Union Election Observation Mission (2016), *The Hashemite Kingdom of Jordan: Parliamentary Election 20 September 2016*, https://www.europarl.europa.eu/cmsdata/212604/Jordan_parliamentary-elections_20-September-2016_EU-EOM-report.pdf (accessed on 6 May 2021). [23]

Hayat Center-Rased (2020), *Rased for Government Performance Monitoring Issues: Its First Report on Al-Khasawneh's Government*, http://www.hayatcenter.org/uploads/2020/10/20201012173747en.pdf (accessed on 31 May 2021). [34]

Hogg, A. and R. Hoodess (2018), *The Business Case for Protecting Civic Rights*, The B Team, http://bteam.niceandserious.com/assets/reports/The-Business-Case-for-Protecting-Civic-Rights.pdf (accessed on 5 May 2021). [8]

ILO (2012), *Macroeconomic policies and employment in Jordan: Tackling the paradox of job-poor growth*, International Labour Organizaton, Employment Sector, Employment Policy Department, https://www.ilo.org/wcmsp5/groups/public/---ed_emp/documents/publication/wcms_191243.pdf (accessed on 28 May 2021). [31]

Institute, I. (ed.) (2020), *Public Opinion Survey: Residents of Jordan November 14 – 22, 2019*, Center for Insights in Survey Research, https://www.iri.org/sites/default/files/jordan_scrubbed_slides_3.27.20_1.pdf (accessed on 6 May 2021). [18]

IPU (2018), *Youth participation in national parliaments: 2018*, Inter-Parliamentary Union, https://www.ipu.org/resources/publications/reports/2018-12/youth-participation-in-national-parliaments-2018 (accessed on 22 April 2020). [38]

Kao, K. and E. Karmel (2020), "The pandemic compromised Jordan's parliamentary elections", *The Washington Post*, https://www.washingtonpost.com/politics/2020/11/20/pandemic-compromised-jordans-parliamentary-elections/ (accessed on 3 May 2021). [35]

Kathrin, T. (2018), *Civic Engagement in the Middle East and North Africa*, Arab Barometer. [36]

Kayyali, A. (2020), *Jordan's Stubborn Insistence on "Business As Usual"*, https://carnegieendowment.org/sada/83232 (accessed on 3 June 2021). [6]

Luck, T. (2019), *Jordan's youth want civil service jobs, despite 10-year waiting list | The National*, The National News, https://www.thenationalnews.com/world/jordan-s-youth-want-civil-service-jobs-despite-10-year-waiting-list-1.856185 (accessed on 28 May 2021). [32]

Ma'ayeh, S. and R. Sweis (2021), *Jordan's 2020 Parliamentary Election: Settling for the Status Quo*, Konrad Adenauer Stiftung, https://www.kas.de/documents/279984/280033/Elections+Article.pdf/4504ba80-43e8-1e18-c5ef-0fd525b30e01?version=1.1&t=1613472770769 (accessed on 6 May 2021). [24]

Manning, N. and K. Edwards (2014), "Does civic education for young people increase political participation? A systematic review", *Educational Review*, Vol. 66/1, pp. 22-45, http://dx.doi.org/10.1080/00131911.2013.763767. [29]

Matasick, C., C. Alfonsi and A. Bellantoni (2020), "Governance responses to disinformation : How open government principles can inform policy options", *OECD Working Papers on Public Governance*, No. 39, OECD Publishing, Paris, https://doi.org/10.1787/d6237c85-en (accessed on 9 June 2021). [15]

Milton-Edwards, B. (2018), "Marginalized youth: Toward an inclusive Jordan", *Brookings Doha Center*, https://www.brookings.edu/research/marginalized-youth-toward-an-inclusive-jordan/ (accessed on 3 May 2021). [2]

Murphy, K. (2004), *The role of trust in nurturing compliance: A study of accused tax avoiders*, Springer, http://dx.doi.org/10.1023/B:LAHU.0000022322.94776.ca. [4]

National Democratic Institute (2015), "Jordan", in National Democratic Institute (ed.), *Voter Registration in the Middle East and North Africa: Select Case Studies*, National Democratic Institute, https://www.ndi.org/Voter-Registration-MENA-Report (accessed on 11 May 2021). [26]

OECD (2021), *Good Practice Principles for Data Ethics in the Public Sector*, https://www.oecd.org/gov/digital-government/good-practice-principles-for-data-ethics-in-the-public-sector.pdf (accessed on 5 May 2021). [11]

OECD (2020), *Engaging Citizens in Jordan's Local Government Needs Assessment Process*, OECD Public Governance Reviews, OECD Publishing, Paris, https://dx.doi.org/10.1787/c3bddbcb-en. [20]

OECD (2020), *Governance for Youth, Trust and Intergenerational Justice: Fit for All Generations?*, OECD Public Governance Reviews, OECD Publishing, Paris, https://dx.doi.org/10.1787/c3e5cb8a-en. [1]

OECD (2020), *How's Life? 2020: Measuring Well-being*, OECD Publishing, Paris, https://dx.doi.org/10.1787/9870c393-en. [25]

OECD (2020), *Innovative Citizen Participation and New Democratic Institutions: Catching the Deliberative Wave*, OECD Publishing, Paris, https://dx.doi.org/10.1787/339306da-en. [19]

OECD (2020), "Learning remotely when schools close: How well are students and schools prepared? Insights from PISA", http://www.oecd.org/coronavirus/en/. [13]

OECD (2020), *Supporting Open Government at the Local Level in Jordan*, OECD, Paris, https://www.oecd.org/gov/open-government/supporting-open-government-at-the-local-level-in-jordan.pdf (accessed on 3 June 2021). [41]

OECD (2020), *Youth and COVID-19: Response, Recovery and Resilience*, OECD Publishing, Paris, https://read.oecd-ilibrary.org/view/?ref=134_134356-ud5kox3g26&title=Youth-and-COVID-19-Response-Recovery-and-Resilience (accessed on 4 July 2020). [42]

OECD (2019), *Institutions Guaranteeing Access to Information: OECD and MENA Region*, OECD Publishing, Paris, https://dx.doi.org/10.1787/e6d58b52-en. [10]

OECD (2019), *Recommendation of the Council on Public Service Leadership and Capability*, OECD/LEGAL/0445, http://legalinstruments.oecd.org (accessed on 28 June 2020). [33]

OECD (2018), *Education for Integrity: Teaching on anticorruption, values and the rule of law*, https://www.oecd.org/governance/ethics/education-for-integrity-web.pdf (accessed on 12 May 2021). [28]

OECD (2018), *Engaging Young People in Open Government: A communication guide*, OECD Publishing, Paris, https://www.oecd.org/mena/governance/Young-people-in-OG.pdf (accessed on 23 July 2020). [40]

OECD (2018), *Youth Stocktaking Report*, https://www.oecd.org/gov/youth-stocktaking-report.pdf (accessed on 30 January 2020). [9]

OECD (2017), *Recommendation of the Council on Open Government*, OECD/LEGAL/0438, http://legalinstruments.oecd.org (accessed on 30 June 2020). [39]

OECD (2017), *Recommendation of the Council on Public Integrity*, https://legalinstruments.oecd.org/en/instruments/OECD-LEGAL-0435. [27]

OECD (2017), *Towards a New Partnership with Citizens: Jordan's Decentralisation Reform*, OECD Public Governance Reviews, OECD Publishing, Paris, https://dx.doi.org/10.1787/9789264275461-en. [21]

OECD (2017), *Trust and Public Policy: How Better Governance Can Help Rebuild Public Trust*, OECD Public Governance Reviews, OECD Publishing, Paris, https://dx.doi.org/10.1787/9789264268920-en. [5]

OECD (2013), *Government at a Glance 2013*, OECD Publishing, Paris, https://dx.doi.org/10.1787/gov_glance-2013-en. [3]

OECD (2021 forthcoming), *Citizens' Voice in Jordan*. [16]

Rased (2020), *Final Report on the Outcomes of Observing the Jordanian Parliamentary Elections 2020*, https://www.rasedjo.com/ar/publications (accessed on 6 May 2021). [22]

Rothstein, B. (2011), *The quality of government: corruption, social trust, and inequality in international perspective*, The University of Chicago Press, Chicago, IL. [7]

Silver, L. et al. (2019), *Mobile Connectivity in Emerging Economies*, Pew Research Center, https://www.pewresearch.org/internet/2019/03/07/mobile-connectivity-in-emerging-economies/ (accessed on 3 June 2021). [14]

Stockemer, D. and A. Sundström (2018), "Age representation in parliaments: Can institutions pave the way for the young?", *European Political Science Review*, Vol. 10/3, pp. 467-490, http://dx.doi.org/10.1017/S1755773918000048. [37]

UNESCO (2017), *Assessing the broader youth environment in Jordan*, UNESCO Amman Office. [30]

Notes

[1] Arab Barometer Wave V.

[2] (Kao and Karmel, 2020[35])

[3] https://www.populationpyramid.net/jordan/2019/

[4] Arab Barometer Wave I.

[5] Arab Barometer Wave V.

[6] A country's score indicates the perceived level of public sector corruption on a scale of 0 (highly corrupt) to 100 (very clean). The Transparency International Index score for Jordan in 2020 was 49.

[7] Arab Barometer Wave V.

[8] Interviews and fact-finding missions conducted by the OECD between 2017 and 2020 in Jordan.

[9] https://haggak.jo/website/.

[10] Data from the Arab Barometer Wave V for 2018-2019 shows that 10% of respondents aged 18-29 reported that they had taken part in peaceful protests in the previous 3 years, compared to 5% of respondents aged 30+ in Jordan.

[11] https://www.conventioncitoyennepourleclimat.fr/

[12] Arab Barometer Wave V.

[13] Arab Barometer Wave V.

[14] Civic education focuses on people's knowledge and understanding of formal institutions and the processes of civic life (such as voting in elections), while citizenship education focuses on knowledge and understanding of opportunities for participation and engagement in both civics and civil society. OECD (2011), How's Life?: Measuring Well-being, OECD Publishing, Paris, https://doi.org/10.1787/9789264121164-en.

[15] http://www.nuorisovaalit.fi/.

[16] https://www.oecd.org/mena/governance/Jordan-mock-elections.pdf.

[17] https://www.euneighbours.eu/en/south/stay-informed/news/jordan-independent-election-commission-and-partners-hold-mock-elections-eu.

[18] OECD calculations based on data from Jordan's Department of Statistics.

[19] OECD calculations based on data from Jordan's Department of Statistics.

[20] https://www.ilo.org/dyn/youthpol/en/equest.fileutils.dochandle?p_uploaded_file_id=171

[21] https://www.populationpyramid.net/jordan/2019/.

[22] The Recommendation defines "stakeholders" as "any interested and/or affected party, including: individuals, regardless of their age, gender, sexual orientation, religious and political affiliations; and institutions and organisations, whether governmental or non-governmental, from civil society, academia, the media or the private sector."

[23] https://www.opengovpartnership.org/wp-content/uploads/2021/04/Jordan_End-of-Term_Report_2016-2018_EN.pdf.

[24] https://www.opengovpartnership.org/wp-content/uploads/2019/01/Jordan_Action-Plan_2018-2020.pdf.

[25] OECD Youth Governance Surveys; https://www.kulturtanken.no/busk.

[26] https://www.mosd.gov.om/index.php/ar/?Itemid=1249&lang=ar-AA.

[27] https://alghad.com.

5 Legal frameworks to empower and protect youth in Jordan

This chapter addresses to what extent key legal frameworks are responsive to young people's needs and provide opportunities for them to participate in public and political life. It analyses minimum age criteria set up to vote and run in elections and those that determine access to employment, education, health, justice and other services that are critical for the transition of youth to an autonomous life. The chapter will benchmark the current criteria in place against the thresholds set across MENA and OECD countries in a constant effort of balancing concerns about protecting and empowering young men and women.

Young people are concerned by government regulations, both in direct and indirect ways. At the macro level, legal frameworks shape youth access to public services and hence opportunities for their personal development in areas such as education and employment, health care and justice. They also have an impact on youth participation in public and social life and their relationship with the state and public institutions. At the micro level, minimum age requirements play a critical role in determining access to public services and the eligibility to vote or run in elections (OECD, 2020[1]). In an effort to strike the balance to protect and empower young people, careful consideration must be given to defining minimum-age thresholds to avoid legal barriers and age-based legal discrimination.

In Jordan, laws are based on the French civil code and Islamic law (Shari'a) and have been influenced by tribal traditions. As a result, the judicial system is divided into civil and religious/Shari'a courts, the latter exercising jurisdiction over personal matters, such as marriage, divorce and inheritance. Laws with a focus on youth are endorsed by the Lower House of Representatives after being reviewed by the Parliamentary Committee for Youth and Sport (UNICEF, 2009[2]).

Defining the rights, roles and responsibilities of youth

The definition of age brackets for "youth" varies significantly across countries and is subject to the respective administrative, social and cultural norms. It defines the beneficiaries (and non-beneficiaries) of government programmes, their access (or non-access) to institutionalised forms of participation. It also shapes the understanding of the rights, roles and responsibilities of this age cohort.

In Jordan, "youth" is defined by the National Youth Strategy 2019-25 as the age group between 12-30 years (Ministry of Youth, 2019[3]), covering a period of 19 years. The age span to define "youth" is 17 years on average across the OECD countries and 13 years on average across most MENA countries[1]. In most MENA countries[2], youth is considered who is 15 years or older, with the exception of Jordan and Mauritania (12 years) and Oman (18 years old). At the upper end, young men and women are considered "youth" until the age of 30 in Jordan, Egypt and Mauritania, whereas it is lower in Algeria, Lebanon, Morocco, Oman and Tunisia (29 years), Syria (25), Qatar, Saudi Arabia and Yemen (24 years) (Youth Policy, 2021[4]).

The Ministry of Youth identifies three sub-groups to provide targeted programmes for different age cohorts: 12-17 years, 19-23 years and 24-30 years. According to the interviews conducted by OECD, 18-year olds are usually not covered specifically as they are usually high-school students in their final year and hence preparing for exams.

National youth laws can help pursue a co-ordinated approach

A youth law or youth act is the most general legislative framework that identifies the main stakeholders and fields of action. It usually extends to state institutions and non-governmental organisations (NGOs) working with and for young people. A youth law or act provides a definition of "youth", a mapping of relevant institutions, the main role of the state vis-à-vis young people, and its relationship with non-governmental (youth) stakeholders (OECD, 2018[5]).

As highlighted by the OECD report "Governance for Youth, Trust and Intergenerational Justice: Fit For All Generations?", as of 2020, 14 OECD countries adopted a national youth law (OECD, 2020[1]). In some OECD countries, youth laws also regulate the support provided by government to non-governmental stakeholders. For instance, in Finland, Luxembourg and Slovenia, the national youth laws feature provisions on the status and functions of the national youth council, including membership conditions (OECD, 2020[1]). Box 5.1 presents the examples of national youth laws in Finland and Colombia.

> **Box 5.1. Examples of national youth laws**
>
> **Finland**
>
> Finland renewed its 1972 Youth Act in 2016. The legislation targets all persons below the age of 29 and covers all aspects of youth work and activities as well as youth policy across all levels of government. It identifies the Ministry of Education and Culture as the primary state authority responsible for the administration, co-ordination and development of the national youth policy, in cooperation with other ministries and central government agencies as well as local authorities, youth associations and other relevant organisations. The Youth Act specifies the key roles and responsibilities of each relevant stakeholders. It also lays out the role of and conditions for the Government in transferring state subsidies to national youth work organisations.
>
> **Colombia**
>
> Colombia adopted a Statutory Law on Youth Citizenship (*Ley Estatutaria de Ciudadanía Juvenil*) in 2013 to establish the institutional framework of youth policy and work and define youth rights. The law created a National Youth System (*Sistema Nacional de la Juventudes*) and defines opportunities for youth participation in the design, implementation and evaluation of youth policy. The Law stipulates that the Presidential Council for Youth (*Consejeria Presidencial para la Juventud*) is in charge of implementing the National Youth Policy. It also lays out the missions of local governments and territorial bodies in the implementation of youth policies and the technical assistance provided by the central level to fulfil their mandate.
>
> Source: (OECD, 2020[1])

Jordan has not formulated a national youth law. Instead, Regulation No. (78) of 2016[3] on "the administrative organisation of the Ministry of Youth" presents the most encompassing regulation on youth affairs. It spells out the organisational structure of the Ministry of Youth, Moreover, law No. (26) of 2018[4] was set up to amend the Higher Council for Youth Law (Law No. 13 of 2005)[5] (Prime Ministry Website, 2016[6]). Law No (26) primarily amended the terminology and replaced references to the Higher Council for Youth by references to the Ministry of Youth, which was created in 2016.

No substantial changes to the law were made, and no clarifications were introduced to identify relevant youth stakeholders in Jordan, to determine their mandates and to create mechanisms for coordination according to the interviews conducted by OECD. From a legal perspective, the mandate of the Ministry of Youth therefore remains unchanged from the legal conditions that regulated the work of the Higher Council for Youth (Prime Ministry Official Website, 2018[7]).

Amendments to Regulation No. (78) of 2016 or the adoption of a national youth law could help address the inherent challenge of multi-level and multi-stakeholder coordination across ministries, non-governmental stakeholders, and international partners in Jordan (Chapter 2 and 3). The findings from the OECD report "Governance for Youth, Trust and Intergenerational Justice: Fit For All Generations?" show that countries with a youth law are less likely to report inter-ministerial co-ordination challenges in the youth field. The need for a more coordinated approach is also recognised by the SWOT analysis conducted for the purpose of the National Youth Strategy 2019-25 (Ministry of Youth, 2019[3]).

Jordan's endorsement of children and youth rights

Jordan was among the first countries in the MENA region along with Egypt and Lebanon to ratify the Convention on the Rights of the Child (CRC) in 1991 (United Nations, 2021[8]), which stipulates the civil, political, economic, social, health and cultural rights of children. It maintains reservations to articles 14, 20 and 21, which concern the freedom of choice of religion and consequently the question of adoption (UN Committee on the Rights of the Child, 2006[9]).

The ratification of the CRC also sets a minimum age of marriage for both gender of 18 years. Nevertheless, challenges persist. OECD analysis highlights that certain provisions in the Personal Status Law (Law No. 36/2010) promote differential treatment of women, including through undermining women's agency in matters of marriage (OECD, 2018[10]). Marriages of girls lower than the age of 18 may be authorised by a the judge in particular cases according to instructions issued by the chief of judges and in case of necessity. According to Girls Not Brides, 8% of girls in Jordan are married before the age of 18 (Girls not brides, 2018[11]). Evidence from the National Department of Statistics suggests that 12% of registered marriages in 2018 concern girls aged 15-17 years (Sharia' courts, 2018[12]). In response to early marriage, the government introduced new regulations regarding exceptional marriages below 18 years in 2017. The regulations determine that the age difference between spouses must not exceed 20 years; otherwise, the consent of the bride is mandatory[6]. (Girls not brides, 2018[11]). Jordan committed to "eliminate all harmful practices, such as child, early and forced marriage" by 2030 in line with target 5.3 of the Sustainable Development Goals (UNICEF, 2021[13]). It also co-sponsored the 2014 UN General Assembly resolution and the 2013 Human Rights Council resolution on child, early and forced marriage.

In light of Jordan's adherence to international agreements and adoption of national laws, further efforts are needed to enforce them. Besides a review of minimum-age requirements, adequate (financial) resources must be allocated to prioritise action in areas, in which young people continue to face challenges in exercising their rights. For instance, in the education sector, the Constitution and the education law guarantee the right to education for all (Ministry of Education, 2018[14]). However, illiteracy rates, school dropout rates and access to higher education continue to disfavour poor households and young people with disabilities. In 2014, it was estimated that almost 4 in 10 youth with disabilities were illiterate, compared to 11% of the total population (Institute of Development Studies, 2018[15]). According to OECD data, economic factors are the central reasons for students to drop out of school[7]. The Education Strategic Plan (2018–2022) commits to provide children who dropped out of school with access to non-formal education programmes (e.g. home schooling) and dropout programmes. However, studies demonstrate that this objective is not reflected in the Ministry's budget (UNICEF, 2019[16]).

The health sector has also made significant efforts over the past decades to deliver more youth-responsive services. Health is not a constitutional right, however, the provision of health care to all Jordanians is stipulated by the amended Public Health Law 47/2008 (UNICEF, 2019[16]). Moreover, the Health Act 83 of 2004 and the civic health insurance guide of 2016 give all children with disabilities as well as all children under six free health services, regardless of their parents' status. Jordan Vision 2025 holds that youth-friendly health care centres should be established to provide targeted mental health services. From the age of six to 18, young people are covered as long as they are enrolled in education and one of their parents is registered with a public insurance. After the age of 18, women are more likely to be insured than men as they are covered automatically by their parents' insurance until they are married in case they are not working. On the other hand, young male students between 18-25 years are covered as long as they are enrolled in higher education or until they are 25 years (Ministry of Health, 2016[17]).

Although youth are defined as key actors in the development process in the National Strategy for Health Sector in Jordan (2015-2019) and the National Reproductive Health Strategy (2013-2017), there is no recognition of their specific health needs nor precise targets for them as a distinct group (OECD, 2018[18]). Children with disabilities face additional challenges as three in ten were not covered by free insurance services according to estimates in 2017 (Institute of Development Studies, 2018[15]).

Minimum-age requirements in Jordan

Minimum-age requirements are common in diverse fields such as compulsory education, access to employment, marriageable age, criminal responsibility, access to justice or certain health services. They also regulate the voting age and age to run as candidate in national and subnational elections. Minimum-age requirements must strike a balance between the need to protect and the aim to empower young men and women, while avoiding unwanted legal barriers and age-based discrimination.

As in most MENA and OECD countries, the age of majority in Jordan is 18 years as per the Jordanian Civil Code (Article 43 of 1976). Custodianship is given by law to the natural mother while the father remains the legal guardian of the child until age 18. Figure 5.1 presents minimum age requirements in Jordan compared to the average of OECD countries in key areas. It demonstrates that the most significant differences exist in terms of young people's opportunity to run for elected office and the age of criminal responsibility.

Figure 5.1. Minimum age requirements in Jordan compared to OECD average, 2021

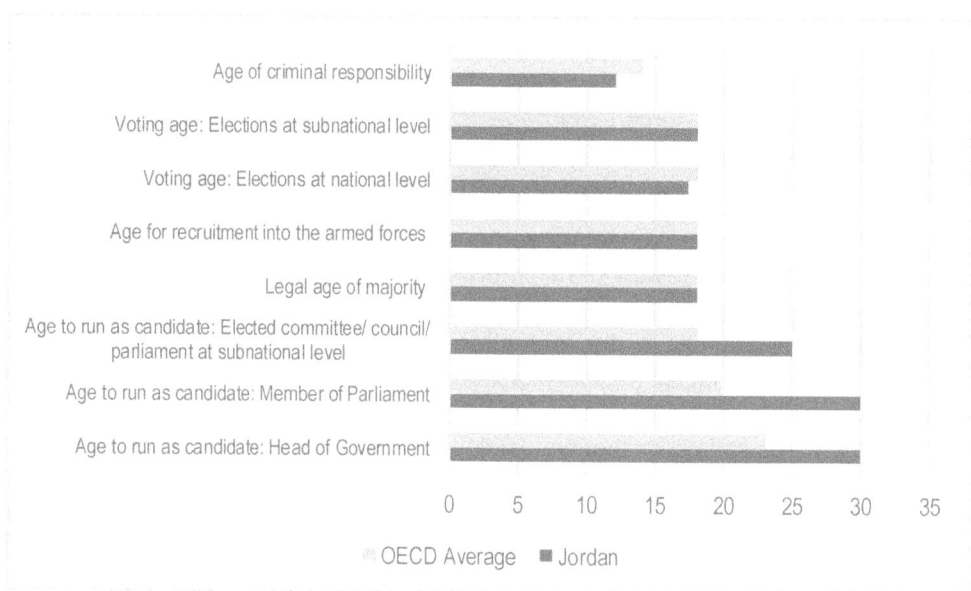

Note: for OECD average the findings are based on 17 to 19 (depending on answer option) OECD government entities in charge of youth affairs.
Source: (AlRai Centre for Studies, 2011[19]) (IFES, 2016[20]) (OECD, 2020[1]) (Ministry of Social Develoment, 2021[21]) (Independent Election Commission, 2021[22])

The next sections will discuss existing minimum age criteria in Jordan in greater detail, in core areas such as employment, health, access to justice services and public and political participation.

Legal safeguards to protect youth in the labour market

Jordan has undertaken efforts to protect young people in the employment sector. Jordan was among the first countries to ratify the conventions by the International Labour Organisation (ILO) addressing child labour, including the Minimum Age Convention Number 138 of 1973 (C138) and the Worst Forms of Child Labour Convention number 182 of 1999 (C182). According to Article 73 of the Labour Law, the minimum age for work[8] in Jordan is 16 years[9] (Ministry of Labour, 2016[23]) (ILO, 2018[24]).

In Jordan, like in most OECD countries, the school leaving age[10] of 16 years is identical with the minimum-age required to engage in part-time work, which shall ensure a smooth transition from education to employment[11] (Ministry of Education, 2020[25]). The minimum age required to work full-time and in hazardous employment[12] is 18 in line with the age required to dispose of own income (ILO, 2020[26]). A person below 18 years requires a guardian to sign an employment contract on his or her behalf (United Nations, 2021[27]).

To protect young workers, Articles 74 and 75 of the Labour Law identify a number of restrictions for working minors (below 18 years). Among others, minors are not allowed to work for more than six hours per day and must be granted at least one-hour breaks after every four consecutive working hours. Their employment is also prohibited between eight o'clock in the evening and six o'clock in the morning and on all public and religious holidays and weekly holidays (ILO, 2020[26]).

A ministerial order, adopted in 2011, shall protect the health and safety of younger employees by determining types of hazardous employment and activities that are prohibited for youth under the age of 18 years (e.g. working in confined places; activities requiring severe physical effort, activities exposed to dust, fiber, fumes, smoke, inflammable materials, extreme temperature, etc.) (ILO, 2011[28]). The Labour Law also stipulates equal access to minimum wages for all workers above 18, which is set at JOD 260 (USD 367) as of 2021 (The Jordan Times, 2021[29]).

Despite these efforts, ILO data from 2016 demonstrates that challenges prevail. For instance, according to the study child labour "remains a matter of grave concern with a significant number of children employed in potentially hazardous jobs", which is estimated to concern around 70,000 children (ILO, 2016[30]).

Promoting access to health services for all ages

In Jordan, young people's access to healthcare, medical advice and counselling for reproductive health services is linked to specific age-based requirements. The minimum age of consent to seek independent medical advice is 18 years. For adolescents younger than 18 years, the Personal Status law No. (15) of 2019 requires parents to cover financially the treatment of their children. For medical treatments and surgeries, the minimum age of consent is also 18 years (General Ifta Department, 2019[31]).

The public health system in Jordan grants access to health insurance to any Jordanian above 18 years paying yearly contributions to the system of JOD 50-75 (USD 71-106) (Ministry of Health, 2016[17]). Confidential testing and treatment for sexually transmitted diseases is legally possible from the age of 18 years. In OECD countries, the minimum age to benefit from medical advice and counselling for reproductive health services ranges from age 12 to 18. In terms of access to mental health services and facilities, there is no specific legislation in place. The General Health Act regulates access to mental health services but does not set any age restriction (WHO, 2011[32]).

In 2008, Jordan adopted the Family Protection Law No. 6 of 2008 to protect the victims of domestic violence of all ages. The law sets out the administrative mechanisms and regulatory provisions to provide support to and protection of victims (Ministry of Social Development, 2008[33]). The law was amended in 2017 to facilitate access to medical services and shelter with the consent of the survivor and in coordination with the Ministry of Social Development (UNESCWA, 2019[34]). Institutionally, the Family Protection Department, created in 1998, is in charge of protecting survivors and victims of child abuse, domestic violence and sexual assaults (Journal of Humanity and Social Sciences, 2019[35]).

Juvenile justice and youth access to justice services

Jordan revised laws with the aim to strengthen the rights of youth in the justice and criminal system. In accordance with the age of majority, the juvenile law in Jordan applies until the age of 18 years. At the age of 12 years, youth are liable for criminal prosecution, compared to an average of 14.5 years in OECD countries (OECD, 2020[1]). In 2014, the Juvenile law No. 32 was revised. Besides raising the minimum age of criminal responsibility from 7 to 12 years, the law encourages the adoption of a rehabilitation-oriented approach to juvenile justice by prioritising alternatives to detention and diversion from the legal system (Ministry of Social Develoment, 2021[21]) (ILO, 2014[36]). The law also regulates that adolescents between

12 and 18 years who are in conflict with the law shall access to juvenile education institutions and rehabilitation institutions and centres under the responsibility of the Ministry of Social Development (UNICEF, 2018[37]).

Youth participation and representation in political life

In 2016, the Law on the "Election of the House of Representatives" (Law 6/2016) was adopted with the objective to make voting easier and more accessible, including for youth, by modifying voter registration from a voluntary system to the automatic registration of all citizens (OECD, 2018[18]). The Interpretation Bureau clarified that citizens who completed 17 years and 90 days before the Election Day were eligible to vote. As result, the number of eligible voters in the 2016 general elections almost doubled, from 2.2 million in 2013 to 4.1 million, increasing first-time young voters by approximately 200,000 (IFES, 2016[20]). Moreover, at the age of 18 years, young people are eligible for joining and forming political parties (Law 39/2015), and creating and joining associations[13] (Law 51/2008 and its amendments in Law 22 of 2009) (Ministry of Social Development, 2021[38]) (AlRai Centre for Studies, 2011[19]) (Ministry of Social Development, 2009[39]).

Table 5.1 provides an overview of the most relevant laws that regulate the participation of citizens in Jordan, including youth, in public and political life.

Table 5.1. Legal frameworks stipulating minimum ages for political participation in Jordan, 2021

Elections Law:	Law 6/2016 holds that citizens aged 17 years as of 90 days prior to election day are eligible to vote and that they must be 30 years and above to run for parliamentary elections
Political Parties Law:	Law 39/2015 stipulates that youth aged 18 years and above can join and/or found political parties.
Municipalities Law:	Law 41/2015 holds that voting in municipal councils elections requires a minimum age of 18 (article 39/A) whereas candidates must be at least 25 years old (article 40/A).
Associations Law:	According to Law 51/2008 and amendments in Law 22/2009, youth must be 18 years or older to found an association.
Public Gatherings Law:	Law 7/2004 and amendments in Law 5/2011 do not stipulate a minimum age required to organise public gatherings after informing the Governor 48 hours in advance.

Source: (Commission, 2021[40]) (Official Gazette, 2021[41])

The legal voting age for national elections in Jordan is aligned with the minimum age required in most MENA and OECD economies with the exception of Austria (16), Greece (17) and the Palestinian Authority (17). In contrast, the age required to run for elected office in Jordan is considerably higher, even in regional comparison. To run as candidate for national parliament, citizens must be 30 years or older, exceeding the OECD average of 19.8 years (OECD, 2018[42]). Across the MENA region, the minimum age required to present oneself as candidate in national elections is lower in most economies, including in the Palestinian Authority (28 years), Lebanon and Mauritania (25 years), and Tunisia (24 years) (Figure 5.2).

Similarly, at the subnational level, candidates must be 25 years or older to be eligible to run for local councils (Municipalities Law 41/2015, article 40/A), exceeding the required minimum age in all OECD and most MENA economies. Only in Lebanon and Mauritania, the minimum age also stands at 25 years to run in local elections.

Figure 5.2. Minimum age requirements in political life across selected MENA economies, 2020

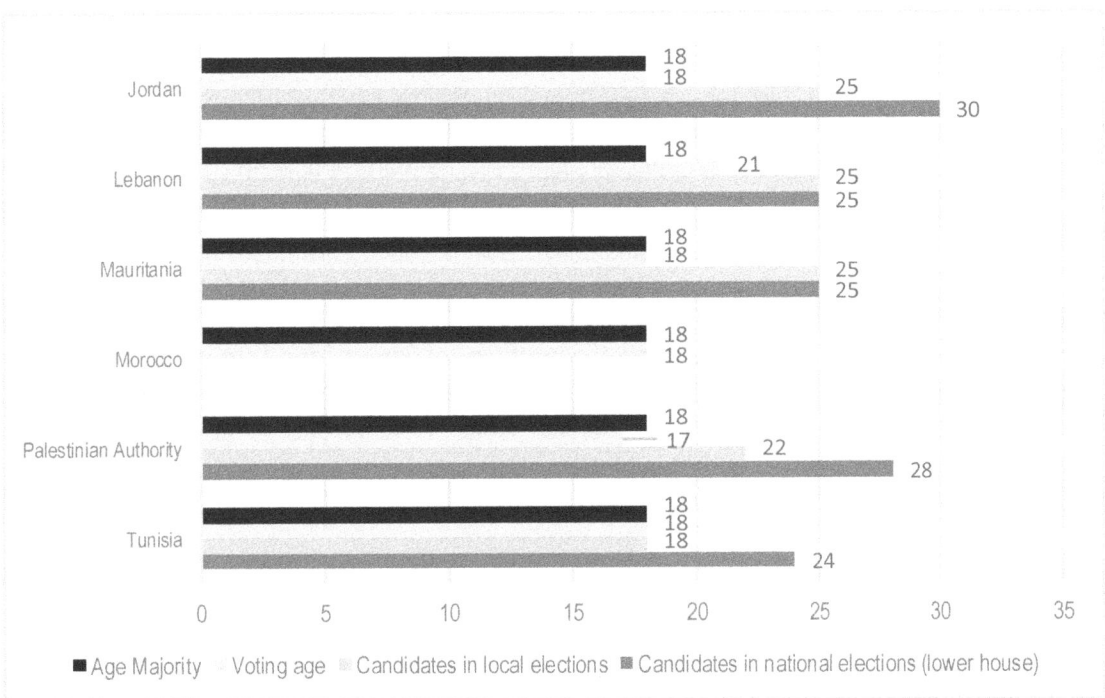

Source: OECD (2020), Youth Empowerment in the MENA region.

In 2011, the Royal Constitutional Review Committee issued a recommendation to reduce the age required to run in parliamentary elections to 25 years in order to "reinforce the role of youth in public and parliamentary life". However, this call has not resulted in a reform of the legal frameworks (OECD, 2018[18]). This criteria risks excluding a large share of the population, as youth aged between 25-30 years represent approximately 10% of the population in Jordan[14] (UNICEF, 2020[43]).

To encourage young people's participation in political life, lowering the minimum age alone is unlikely to immediately result in a higher number of young people in political positions (Chapter 4). Such measures must be accompanied by addressing other structural barriers, for instance the financial burden of running a campaign. In Jordan, candidates are required to pay a JOD 500 (USD 705) registration fee and each list must pay a refundable collateral of JOD 2000 (USD 2821), which is unaffordable for most youth. A holistic approach to must also take into account the social norms and perceptions that may favour older over younger contestants in elections due to the presumed lack experience and networks. According to the interviews conducted by OECD with representatives from youth-led organisations, the presumed lack of social capital among young people and the dominance of personal connections ("wasta") are considered key barriers to youth participation in politics.

Reforms undertaken by the Government of Jordan to enhance the participation of women in political life provide important insights to ensure a more inclusive access for all groups in society, including the youth cohort. A quota of 20% for women was introduced for municipal council seats in 2007, which was raised to 25% in 2011. In 2015, the Municipalities Law (Law number 41 of 2015) established a new structure for municipal governance, by stipulating the creation of directly elected local and governorate councils, as well as municipal councils. The law features a 25% quota for women in both local and municipal councils and introduced a 10% quota for women in governorate councils (OECD, 2018[10]).

Addressing legal discrimination of young women

Young women are often affected disproportionally by legal barriers enshrined in laws, preventing them from passing on their nationality to their children and spouses, or affecting a (young) woman's right to marry, divorce, and to inherit. Jordan ratified the Convention on the Elimination of All Forms of Discrimination against Women in 1992. However, it maintains reservation to article 9 (relative to the nationality of children) (United Nations Treaty Collection, 2021[44]) and article 16 (relative to the rights and responsibilities during marriage, as parents, regarding professions and occupation) (UNICEF, 2009[2]).

For instance, according to the Jordanian Nationality Law of 1954, Jordanian women married to non-Jordanian men do not have the right to pass their nationality to their spouses nor to their children, unlike men. According to the Personal Status Law number 36 of 2010, women who get married for the first time are required to obtain consent from their male guardians to get married, otherwise, the marriage is prohibited (Article 14 of the Personal Status Law of 2010). Women like men can include in their marriage contracts specific conditions including the right to work, travel a nd apply for unilateral divorce (Article 37 of the Personal Status Law of 2010) (Jordan, n.d.[45]).

Recommendations

- **Clearly defining the responsibilities and mandates** of state and non-state institutions working with and for young people, for instance by amending law No. (78) of 2016 or drafting a national youth law to address fragmentation in the delivery of policies, programmes and services for youth.
- **Conducting a review of minimum-age requirements across public services areas** against international benchmarks to identify barriers for youth to access them.
- **Considering lowering minimum age requirements** for candidates for national and subnational elections in line with recommendations by the Royal Constitutional Review Committee.
- **Enforcing laws identifying minimum age requirements** to protect young men and women from harm, for instance working full-time and in hazardous employment.

References

AlRai Centre for Studies (2011), *Youth and Political Parties in Jordan*, http://www.alraicenter.com/User_Site/Site/View_Articlear.aspx?type=2&ID=352. [19]

Commission, I. (2021), *Independent Election Commission - Jordan*, https://iec.jo/en. [40]

General Ifta Department, J. (2019), *Homepage*, https://aliftaa.jo/ShowContent.aspx?Id=205#.YJkZjbUzY2w. [31]

Girls not brides (2018), *Less talk, more action to address child marriage in emergencies*, https://www.girlsnotbrides.org/articles/less-talk-end-child-marriage-conflict/. [11]

IFES (2016), *Elections in Jordan, 2016 Parliamentary Elections*. [20]

ILO (2020), *National Labour Law Profile: Jordan*.	[26]
ILO (2018), *Child Labour in Jordan*.	[24]
ILO (2016), *Child labour doubles in Jordan since 2007 – Survey*, https://www.ilo.org/beirut/media-centre/news/WCMS_510750/lang--en/index.htm.	[30]
ILO (2014), *Law No. 32 of 2014 concerning Juvenile Law*, https://www.ilo.org/dyn/natlex/natlex4.detail?p_isn=100351&p_lang=en.	[36]
ILO (2013), *Guide to Jordanian Labour Law for the Garment Industry*, https://www.ilo.org/wcmsp5/groups/public/---arabstates/---ro-beirut/documents/publication/wcms_218390.pdf.	[49]
ILO (2011), *Ministerial Order of 2011, concerning occupations that are dangerous or tiring or harmful to the health of youth*.	[28]
Independent Election Commission, J. (2021), *Homepage*, https://www.iec.jo/.	[22]
Index Mundi (2020), *Jordan Profile*, https://www.indexmundi.com/jordan/demographics_profile.html.	[46]
Institute of Development Studies (2018), *The current situation of persons with disabilities in Jordan*.	[15]
Jordan, P. (n.d.), *Jordanian Personal Status Law No. 36 of 2010*.	[45]
Journal of Humanity and Social Sciences (2019), *Family Protection Department (FPD) in Jordan: The Legal Arm to Protect Women*.	[35]
Ministry of Education (2020), *Jordan, Ministry of Education*.	[25]
Ministry of Education (2018), *Education Strategic Plan (2018-2022)*.	[14]
Ministry of Health (2016), *Jordan, Civil Health Insurance System Guide and Instructions*.	[17]
Ministry of Labour (2016), *Jordan, National Child Labour Survey*.	[23]
Ministry of Social Develoment (2021), *Jordan, Homepage*.	[21]
Ministry of Social Development (2021), *Law of Associations and its amendments no. 51 of 2008*, http://www.mosd.gov.jo/ui/arabic/.	[38]
Ministry of Social Development (2009), *Jordan, Law No. 22 of 2009*, https://menarights.org/sites/default/files/2016-11/JOR_LawOnSocieties_2009_AR.pdf.	[39]
Ministry of Social Development (2008), *Jordanian Domestic Violence Protection Law No. 6 of 2008*.	[33]
Ministry of Youth (2019), *Jordan, National Youth Strategy (2019-25)*.	[3]
OECD (2020), *Governance for Youth, Trust and Intergenerational Justice: Fit For All Generations?*, OECD.	[1]
OECD (2019), *Key Issues affecting Youth in Jordan*, https://www.oecd.org/countries/jordan/youth-issues-jordan.htm.	[48]

OECD (2018), *Seven key findings from the youth governance survey*, https://www.oecd.org/mena/governance/Seven-key-findings.pdf. [42]

OECD (2018), *Women's Political Participation in Jordan*, https://www.oecd.org/mena/governance/womens-political-participation-in-jordan.pdf. [10]

OECD (2018), *Youth Stocktaking Report*, OECD, https://www.oecd.org/gov/youth-stocktaking-report.htm. [5]

OECD (2018), *Youth Well-being Policy Review of Jordan*, http://oe.cd/42M. [18]

Official Gazette (2021), *Newspaper*, http://www.pm.gov.jo/newspaper. [41]

Prime Ministry Official Website (2018), *Jordan, Homepage*, http://www.pm.gov.jo/newspaperSubjects/5517/5517.html. [7]

Prime Ministry Website (2021), *East Laws*, http://site.eastlaws.com/GeneralSearch/Home/ArticlesTDetails?MasterID=234518&related. [50]

Prime Ministry Website (2016), *Jordan, Regulation No. (78) of 2016*, https://doc.pm.gov.jo/. [6]

Sharia' courts, J. (2018), *Registered Marriages by Age of Bride and Groom*, http://www.dos.gov.jo/dos_home_a/main/vitality/Marriage_and_Divorce/2018/Marriages8.pdf. [12]

The Jordan Times (2021), *Minimum wage to go up to JD260 at onset of 2021*. [29]

UN Committee on the Rights of the Child (2006), *Consideration of Reports submitted by states parties under article 44 of the convention CRC/C/JOR/3*, http://docstore.ohchr.org/SelfServices/FilesHandler.ashx?enc=6QkG1d%2FPPRiCAghKb7yhsiaA1%2F6olxyVVmNojGiLiCfAgQR6ulgIMgmHRBnYiFGw15cc%2F5ltL1UuJn5iSMaODbn7Ah%2B1NE4GOtB9qL0TopN6viYiBitviRfanoLuBJNv. [9]

UNESCO (2018), *Assessing the broader youth environment in Jordan*, http://www.unesco.org/new/fileadmin/MULTIMEDIA/FIELD/Amman/pdf/Assessing_broader_youth_environment_JOR.pdf. [47]

UNESCWA (2019), *Shelters for Women Survivors of Violence*. [34]

UNICEF (2021), *Sustainable Development Indicators*, https://data.unicef.org/sdgs/country/jor/. [13]

UNICEF (2020), *Jordan*, https://www.unicef.org/jordan/youth#:~:text=Challenges,is%20not%20without%20its%20challenges. [43]

UNICEF (2019), *BUDGET BRIEF 2019 public Education Sector in Jordan*. [16]

UNICEF (2018), *Situation Analysis of Juvenile Justice*. [37]

UNICEF (2009), *JORDAN MENA Gender Equality Profile Status of Girls and Women in the Middle East and North Africa*, UNICEF. [2]

United Nations (2021), *CHAPTER IV HUMAN RIGHTS 11. Convention on the Rights of the Child*, https://treaties.un.org/Pages/ViewDetails.aspx?src=IND&mtdsg_no=IV-11&chapter=4. [8]

United Nations (2021), *Minimum age to join work agreement (No. 138)*, https://www.ohchr.org/EN/pages/home.aspx. [27]

United Nations Treaty Collection (2021), . [44]

WHO (2011), *The assessment of the mental health system in Jordan*. [32]

Youth Policy (2021), *Factsheets*, https://www.youthpolicy.org/. [4]

Notes

[1] MENA countries covered include Algeria, Egypt, Jordan, Lebanon, Mauritania, Morocco, Oman, Qatar, Saudi Arabia, Syria, Tunisia and Yemen.

[2] Youth is considered who is 15 years or older in Algeria, Egypt, Lebanon, Morocco, Qatar, Saudi Arabia, Syria, Tunisia and Yemen, while in Jordan and Mauritania it is 12 years and in Oman it is 18 years.

[3] Regulation No. (78) of 2016 on "the administrative organisation of the Ministry of Youth" spells out its organisational structure and stipulates the creation of the Committee for Planning, Coordination and Follow-up, which assists and advises the Minister in his functions. It is presidated by the Minister and gathers the Secretary-General and the Directors of the National Youth and Sports Fund, Hussein Youth City, the Youth Leadership Centre and up to two directors of the directorates. This regulation replaces the law on "the administrative organisation of the Higher Council for Youth Law No.(30) of 2002 (Prime Ministry Website, 2016[6]).

[4] Law No. (26) of 2018 amends the Higher Council for Youth Law (Law No. 13 of 2005) (Prime Ministry Official Website, 2018[7]). It was published in 2018 on the official portal of the Prime Ministry Office.

[5] The Higher Council for Youth Law No. (13) of 2005 stipulates the mandate, mission, vision and structure of the Higher Council for Youth which was established in 2001 to replace the Ministry of Youth. In 2016, the Higher Council for Youth was replaced by the Ministry of Youth under Regulation No. 78 of 2016 on the administrative organisation of the Ministry, followed by Law No. (26) of 2018 (Prime Ministry Website, 2021[50])

[6] The prospective bride and groom or their respective guardians must both consent to the marriage. (Personal Status Law No. 36 of 2010, arts. 6 and 7, https://tbinternet.ohchr.org/Treaties/CEDAW/Shared%20Documents/JOR/INT_CEDAW_NGO_JOR_26632_E.pdf

[7] OECD database, key issues affecting youth in Jordan (OECD, 2019[48])

[8] A list of 29 hazardous occupations in which children under-18 cannot work was adopted in 1997, which was revised in April 2011 (ILO, 2018[24]). https://www.ilo.org/wcmsp5/groups/public/---arabstates/---ro-beirut/documents/genericdocument/wcms_210566.pdfThe list includes the work that is considered to be harmful to a child's physical, social or psychological development (ILO, 2020[26])

[9] When employing a worker between 16 and 18 years of age, the following documents are required: i) a certified copy of the minor's birth certificate; ii) a certificate of health fitness to perform the required work,

issued by a competent; iii) physician and certified by the Ministry of Health, and iv) written consent of the minor's guardian, (ILO, 2013[49])

[10] The school leaving age is the minimum age at which a person is legally allowed to leave compulsory education, while the employment age is the minimum age at which a person is allowed to take up legal employment either full-time or part-time.

[11] OECD Family database, Social Policy Division, Directorate of Employment, Labour and Social Affairs, https://www.oecd.org/els/family/PF_1_8_Age_threshold_Childhood_to_Adulthood.pdf

[12] Hazardous employment is the work that involves using dangerous machinery and equipment according to the Ministry of Labor (Article 74 of Labour Law No. 8 of 1996) (i.e. explosives; fire, gas; chemicals; underwater work; work in mines; at construction sites etc); (UNESCO, 2018[47])

[13] According to the Associations Law and its amendments No. 51 of 2008 the term "association" refers to any legal entity composed of a group of at least seven persons and is registered in accordance with the provisions of the Associations, aiming to provide services and to carry out activities on a voluntary basis, without targeting to earn profits ot to achieve any benefit for any of its members or for any specific person. The association must not achieve any political goals that fall within the framework or activities of political parties. In terms of eligibility, the members of the association (including the founder) must be Jordanian, at least 18 years old, with a clean criminal record and full legal capacity. Any fundings or donations from outside Jordan must be submitted to the Prime Ministry for approval. The membership of "Private associations" is restricted to a group of three to twenty people. A "closed association" refers to an association whose membership is restricted to one or more persons, and whose financial resources are limited to its founding members, (Ministry of Social Development, 2008[33])

The term "private association" means an association whose membership is restricted to a group of persons whose number is not less than three and not more than twenty. The term "closed association" means an association whose membership is restricted to one or more persons, and whose financial resources are limited to what any founding member provides for the purposes of enabling it to achieve its goals.

[14] Based on population data retrieved from reports by UNICEF and evidence from Index Mundi, youth aged between 25-30 years represent approximately 10.2% of the population in Jordan (i.e. youth under 30 represent 63% of the population and 52.8% are below 25 years) (UNICEF, 2020[43]) (Index Mundi, 2020[46]).

 www.ingramcontent.com/pod-product-compliance
Ingram Content Group UK Ltd.
Pitfield, Milton Keynes, MK11 3LW, UK
UKHW050413240426
12048UKWH00020B/1487